Forty Days and Forty Nights

Brother Ramon studied Theology at Cardiff, Zurich and Edinburgh and is a member of the Anglican Society of St Francis. He was Guardian of Glasshampton Monastery until his departure to explore the hermit life.

Also available from the same author

HEAVEN ON EARTH
A HIDDEN FIRE
DEEPER INTO GOD
SOUL FRIENDS
JACOPONE
LIFE'S CHANGING SEASONS
PRAYING THE BIBLE
PRAYING THE JESUS PRAYER

FORTY DAYS AND FORTY NIGHTS

A guide to spending time alone with God

BROTHER RAMON SSF

Illustrations by Molly Dowell

MarshallPickering

An Imprint of HarperCollinsPublishers

Marshall Pickering is an Imprint of
HarperCollins*Religious*
Part of HarperCollins*Publishers*
77–85 Fulham Palace Road, London W6 8JB

First published in Great Britain
in 1993 by Marshall Pickering

3 5 7 9 10 8 6 4 2

Unless otherwise stated, biblical extracts are taken from the New
International Version of the Bible (NIV) copyright © 1978 by New
York International Bible Society, and are used by permission of the UK
publisher, Hodder & Stoughton.

A catalogue record for this book is available from the British Library

ISBN 0 551 02738-X

Printed and bound in Great Britain by
HarperCollinsManufacturing Glasgow

With gratitude for love and hospitality
to Mother and Sisters of
The Society of the Sacred Cross,
Tymawr, Monmouth

✝

CONTENTS

PROLOGUE

How To Use This Book

I am not presuming that you are going off on a forty-day retreat (chance would be a fine thing!) or that you are going to spend an intensive and extended period of study and prayer in using this book. So let me explain what I have in mind.

The book may be used on a personal or group basis and there may be great variation in its use. It includes under each day the theme with its Scripture, prayer and reflection. This is followed by a three-question response in which you are invited to use your spiritual journal or notebook, and a closing quotation.

It is ideal to take with you on retreat or holiday, or you may set aside "an hour for God" for a period of forty days as a special time for the Lord to speak.

If used in a group, particular themes may be selected or some themes linked together, and various people may be chosen to present their "homework" from the response sections at the following week's meeting, with recommendations from them for particular action arising from a theme. But of course there is no reason why you may not use it as a devotional and study book at your own leisure, or with a friend.

A word about retreats. I prepared *Heaven on Earth** primarily as a retreat book, and it was so well received that this present book is a result of such enthusiasm. Here I seek to share my life with you in such a way that it will stimulate

* *Heaven on Earth* contains an extensive section on making a retreat with suggested timetable, diet, meditation method and practice of mindfulness.

ix

your own growth in prayer and spark off new ways of understanding and sharing God's love with others.

If you have never been on retreat I would encourage you to get off for at least a few days – a week if possible. Details and addresses can be found in *Vision* magazine of the National Retreat Movement, or you can enquire at your local convent or monastic house. There are scores of monasteries and retreat houses offering conducted retreats of all kinds, or as much quiet and space as you need for a private retreat.

I have used a hut, a caravan, a tent (risky!), a stone cottage and many religious houses for retreat – a time to be totally available for God, away from demands, telephone, responsibilities. You need time to unwind before you get into the rhythm of it, especially if you are used to a busy and active life. If you are making your first retreat it is well to have someone on hand to refer to, for the Lord often uses the silence and receptivity of a retreat to touch the heart. That is why it is advisable to share your first retreat with others and to stay in a retreat house where a life of daily worship and counsel is available.

It doesn't matter what your denomination or church background is, you will be welcome at a retreat house, though it is a good idea to check about receiving communion. We are living in days when evangelicals and catholics are mixing more freely and are involved together in social and caring concerns as a direct result of their commitment to Christ.

In using this book we are going on a journey and you will need a Bible, a blank exercise book (or your spiritual journal) and a prayerful, willing heart. Proceed as follows:

1 Find a quiet place and settle down, affirming the presence of God;
2 Turn up the Bible passage and read it through slowly;

3 Spend a minute in silence, then say the set prayer followed by another minute of silence;

4 Read the material under the heading "Reflection";

5 Go through the "Response" section, using your journal to answer any questions, to record your feelings about the theme, and how you intend to act upon any task or challenge set before you;

6 Read the final quotation, taking note how it brings out some aspect of the theme;

7 Write into your journal any comments or questions of your own about the theme, to be used in further exploration.

God has spoken to me through these themes and I believe he will speak to you. So if you are geared up, let's go!

BROTHER RAMON SSF

DAY ONE

Inviting

SCRIPTURE: John 1:29–51. "Come and see."

Prayer

Lord Jesus Christ:
Sometimes, when you speak your words of loving invitation,
I refuse to hear, and turn the other way. Am I afraid that
your call involves a hard and disciplined way of sorrow and
discipleship which I shall not be able to bear?
Grant today that, hearing your word, my heart may be
touched, my mind enlightened and my will moved to respond
with great joy, trusting you wholly for the outcome;
For your dear name's sake. Amen.

Reflection

I love the old story of a hermit who lived in a cave on a
hill above a Celtic village. He was renowned for his wisdom
which was invariably mixed with a challenge to a wholesome
and positive change of life, and was often visited by the
village folk at times of perplexity.

Two of the wiseacre village lads one day decided to play
a joke on him and catch him out. They planned to call for
him outside the cave, one of them holding a small living bird
behind his back, and ask him the question: "Father, is this
bird in my hand alive or dead?"

If he said it was dead the boy would open his hand and

1

send it flying into the heavens. But if he said it was alive the boy would crush it to prove the old man wrong.

They ascended the hill and called until the hermit appeared. "Father," said one of the lads, "I have a small bird in my hand. Is it alive or dead?"

There was silence. The old man fixed him with his gaze. Eventually he chuckled and said: "Well, boys – it all depends on you!"

I don't pretend to any profound wisdom, being a pilgrim on the way myself. But this story appeals to me because its ethos has to do with the path of wisdom and self-knowledge which is part of the hermit tradition which I have dipped into over the past decade and am now living somewhat more seriously.

The story also gives out a challenge and an invitation to you to share in some of the simple and yet profound things which belong to such a life – to step inside the life with me as I talk to myself and to you in the presence of the One who calls us both into a deeper life of prayer and love.

I have chosen the title *Forty Days and Forty Nights* because in the Bible this is not so much a literal period of time (though it may also be that), but a creative period which spells out mercy and judgement, and which is always meant for the good of those who participate in it. How will sharing such a period with a brother who is experimenting with the hermit life be of value to a man or woman caught up in the busy world of family, household, career, ambition and politics? Well, as the old hermit said: "It all depends on you."

The creative period of forty themes in this book contains positive and negative factors, calling for personal and communal reflection. Issues of psychological and spiritual maturity are faced, pain and conflict being part of the process but not unmixed with joy and enthusiasm – and a dash of humour.

The strange thing is that living in solitude can deepen your love for other human beings – especially if you are a gregarious character like me. But it is also a source of humility as you look at yourself as you really are, and it may increase the longing to add to the compassion needed in our poor world.

One of the things that this book says is that every Christian, indeed every human being, needs a pool of solitude in his or her life – and children are included in such an evaluation. It is my own childhood which has propelled me into this solitude. If I had not given heed to my childhood and begun to learn again those lessons which I was first taught in infancy and boyhood I would not be testing the hermit life now.

I say "testing" because I am still new to the game. I spent six months in a hut in Dorset in 1982, six months at the tip of Lleyn Peninsula in a primitive stone cottage in 1983/4, and am well into my second year in a caravan in an enclosed plum orchard surrounded by fields and woodland some miles from Monmouth as I write today.

I am on pilgrimage as we all are, and for the present I am participating in a life which means prayer in solitude. This may go on for many years – perhaps the rest of my life will be spent pursuing such a vocation. Or it may continue for a year or two more and the Lord may open up another form of life and ministry as a Franciscan friar. I don't know. But I don't *need* to know the future but live in the present moment and trust the Lord who has led me thus far and will lead me on.

That is why this invitation comes to you, for if you will listen and talk back to me in your mind and heart in our common life in God, then the sad, funny, ridiculous, practical and spiritual reflections set down here will engage your attention and cause you to take your own pilgrimage more seriously and more joyously.

You are not *compelled* to make such a journey with me,

but you are *invited* – and encouraged. And the result? Well, by the grace of God, and as the old hermit said: "It all depends on you!"

Response

* Is there an area of your life where you have felt the call of Jesus to go deeper, to launch out in faith, to trust him more?

* Have you found a willingness or a reluctance to respond to his invitation?

* Imagine you are one of the disciples in today's reading. Write down how you may have responded to the call of Jesus.

Love's Invitation

If Love should count you worthy and should deign
One day to seek your door and be your guest,
Pause! ere you draw your bolt and bid him rest
If in your old content you would remain.
For not alone he enters; in his train
Are angels of the mists, the lonely quest,
Dreams of the unfulfilled and unpossessed,
And sorrow and life's immemorial pain.
He wakes desires you never may forget,
He shows you stars you never saw before,
He makes you share with him forevermore
The burden of the world's divine regret.
How wise you were to open not, and yet,
How poor if you should turn him from your door.

S. R. LYSAGHT

DAY TWO

Preparing

SCRIPTURE: Exodus 24:1–18. The glory of the Lord

Prayer

Covenant God of Israel:
You have always called your chosen servants to the
mountain, the wilderness and the desert for humbling,
revelation and restoration.
Give me grace to feel myself part of that great company of
those called into closer fellowship with you;
Show me your glory, confirm in me your covenant love,
and restore to me the joy of your salvation;
Through Jesus Christ my Lord. Amen.

Reflection

I want to pause at the outset of our journey today to locate
and point up the meaning of the mystical number *forty* in
the Bible. In Rumer Godden's powerful novel *In This House
of Brede*, one of the Benedictine nuns states it succinctly:
"Forty, always forty," said Sister Scholastica, "Christmas,
Lent, Paschaltide, forty days in the wilderness, it's a mystic
number."

I certainly feel a mystic pull towards solitude and prayer,
and such a thing is not confined to the religious life of monk,
nun, priest or minister. It is part of the life of every Christian.
An area of solitude is part of the natural inheritance of every
human person. But let's look at the biblical witness.

5

For Moses, the forty days and nights were spent upon Mount Sinai – first of all to gaze upon the revelation of God's glory and splendour in such a measure that his face was transfigured by the dazzling brightness of God's outshining (Exodus 24:1–18; 33:12–22; 34:29–35). Secondly he received from God the revelation of the Law contained in the Ten Commandments (Exodus 34:1–28). Thirdly, he prostrated himself in intercession, pleading for sinful Israel and bearing the burden of the people of God in prayer (Deuteronomy 9:25–29). These were creative periods for Moses and for the people but they demanded face-to-face confrontation with the divine glory and the divine judgement.

Another aspect of a creative period of forty days and nights is one of exploration and pilgrimage, as we find in Numbers 13:1–25. Moses sent out twelve men (another mystical number) from the twelve tribes to explore the land of Canaan for this duration of time. Reading this story reminds us that we are on our way from the Egypt of our old sinful lives, pilgrims in the wilderness of the world with our eyes set on the heavenly Canaan. But while our feet are planted necessarily and firmly in the world's wilderness, our hearts must yearn for the heavenly country where our true citizenship lies, and we must explore the life of heaven while living on earth (Philippians 3:20). The whole eleventh chapter of the Letter to the Hebrews is our pattern on such a pilgrimage, and if we faint on the way we are sustained by the renewing grace of the Holy Spirit.

Elijah learned continually the value of periods of solitude in his prophetic ministry, sometimes as an antidote to physical, mental and spiritual exhaustion. At one point, running in sheer funk from Jezebel's threats, he made his way into the southern wilderness, fell down under a broom tree and asked God to take his life away – and then fell asleep, exhausted.

The Lord allowed him to sleep then woke him and provided food and drink. The text goes on: "Strengthened by that food, he travelled for forty days and forty nights until he reached Horeb, the mount of God. There he went into a cave and spent the night" (1 Kings 19:8, 9).

The cave, in the mystical tradition, is the depth of the human heart which may become the cave of God's indwelling. It is a terrifying and yet an assuring place. Terrifying, because you have to face the stripped and naked self which you become when confronted by the divine mystery of God's holiness and love; assuring, because with all its dark mystery it is the covenanted trysting place where the soul rests in the bosom of God.

One of the primary things that solitude teaches me is to tremble in God's presence. Living close to nature in surroundings exposing me to the change of seasons in hermit solitude causes a trembling born of both joy and reverential awe. The Desert Fathers espoused no sentimental concept of an easy-going God, nor any philosophical view of a divine Absolute. They were confronted with the living God of Scripture and desert before whom they fell down in fear and trembling.

I am not a nature mystic or a sentimental animal-lover roving around springtime fields and woods, penning verses and indulging in vague general benevolence for the human race while absenting myself from my fellow human beings and from the hurry and grime of the marketplace. I live in fear and trembling because of God's holy love and because of his loving holiness.

Forty days and forty nights of judgement are revealed in the flood of Noah (Genesis 7:4); in the judgement against the ten spies who refused the challenge of the exploration of Canaan (Numbers 14:33–35); and in the first preaching of Jonah when he cried against the sin of the great city, saying: "Forty days more and Nineveh will be destroyed" (Jonah 3:4).

But the clouds of God's judgement are always lined with mercy, and if God calls you and me into a forty days and nights of judgement and purging it will always be in the nature of chastisement and correction, in order that his mercy may abound all the more. But judgement, because of our hardness of heart and perversity, is often the only way through to mercy, and there can be no evasion.

The forty days and nights of Jesus' temptation in the wilderness, surrounded by the powers of darkness and wild animals, can be a creative pattern for our journey during the forty days of Lent (Matthew 4:1–11; Mark 1:12f.; Luke 4:1–13). The hymn on the theme set to the tune *Aus der Tiefe* (Out of the Depths) may sound solemn, but it is only those who are willing to follow into such depths who can emerge into the resurrection glory of the One who has conquered death and hell:

> Forty days and forty nights
>   You were fasting in the wild;
> forty days and forty nights
>   Tempted, and yet undefiled . . .
>
> Keep, O keep us, Saviour dear,
>   Ever constant by Your side
> That with You we may appear
>   At the eternal Eastertide.

And lastly there is a wonderful word for us in Acts 1:3, where Jesus ministers to his disciples after his resurrection, preparing them for courageous witness and proclamation: "For forty days after his death he appeared to them many times in ways that proved beyond doubt that he was alive. They saw him and he talked with them about the Kingdom of God" (GNB). So let us begin.

Response

* Consider that God may be asking you to enter into a period of retreat (brief or extended) with more solitude than previously.

* Will you take steps to find out more information about all kinds of retreats?

* If you discover yourself drawn to such a creative challenge, will you, in spite of fears and apprehensions, talk about it with some experienced person and consider undertaking such an exploration?

The Desert of the Heart

For everyone there is a call into the desert. But few truly respond to that call. Some fail to hear it because their lives are cluttered with schemes, possessions and ambitions which drown the call of the Spirit. Even those who hear the call may then close their ears because they are afraid of facing God in the nakedness of solitude, or because they suspect that God will challenge them with the demands of the divine love. Those who hear and feel an answering yearning deep within their own hearts may be tempted and deflected by the claims of family, career or society which place before the believer the insistent duties of what seems to be the "real world".

But there are some who hear the call clearly, who free themselves from sins, worldly attachments and lesser loves to follow the call into the desert for a confrontation with the living God.

The desert may be a geographic location where the man or woman waits in solitude; it may be a state of mind which is open to new guidance and revelation; it will certainly be a desert of the heart which is the trysting-place where God meets with those who long for him.

9

Listen then for that call which is ever sounding. When its echo reverberates in your heart, give yourself to it in love, for in surrendering to the call of the desert you will be enveloped in that mystery for which you were made — union with the living God.

Part I

BODY

DAY THREE

Beginning

SCRIPTURE: Hebrews 11:8–10. Into the Land of Unknowing

Prayer

Heavenly Father:
You always call your servants onward and upward into more fruitful ways of loving and serving you. Sometimes there are mists on the way and I cannot discern the path ahead. Let me not hold back in doubt or fear but, strengthened by your Holy Spirit, follow on in obedience to the heavenly vision;
Through Jesus Christ my Lord. Amen.

Reflection

I didn't know where it would all lead when I began. The exciting and thrilling love of the Lord was the sprat to catch a mackerel! Indeed, I sometimes feel I would not have begun if I had known then what I know now. But the Lord leads us on in gently ascending paths until our feet begin to tread the higher places. I must admit now that I am afraid, and that perhaps if I knew where it may lead I might again fight shy and draw back. But these feelings co-exist with joy and with the enthusiasm and vision which I have glimpsed in Scripture, in the Fathers of the desert, the Celtic monks and the early Franciscan friars. All these, with many others, are part of this wonderful way of prayer and solitude which it is my privilege to share during this exploration of forty days and forty nights.

God's call into new and unknown dimensions can be scary, but such a call indicates his special love for us, and with the call comes the ability to fulfil the vocation, if we are willing. We must let go the old ways and venture in faith as he leads us.

The mountain to and from which God calls us may not be named Sinai, Carmel, Tabor or Calvary, but it will be our mountain of holiness, surrounded by fire, mists and glory. The same God calls us as called Moses and Elijah of old, and he will be with us as he was with them.

I tell elsewhere the story of how I was first hooked on to the path of prayer and solitude (*A Hidden Fire*, part I; *Deeper into God*, ch. 13). This present part of the journey began in August 1990 when John and Mervyn towed the hermitage caravan, journeying with me from Glasshampton monastery in Worcestershire to the grounds of Tymawr Convent, near Monmouth. We trundled it through the fields down to the plum orchard. The orchard measures nearly 150 × 40 feet and is enclosed by a hedge and trees, the entrance crossed by two metal bars (to keep the sheep out, not me in!).

I stayed in the convent on the night of 28th August, and the next day was the commemoration of the Beheading of St John the Baptist – an appropriate day to begin. I thought it was the Lord's humour. Brother Anselm SSF, representing the Society of St Francis and as my provincial minister, preached the homily at the eucharist. He spoke appropriately of John the Baptist in prison, Peter in prison, Paul and Silas in prison, saying that the latter both sang praises in the prison as he expected I would too.

After receiving communion and the blessing, a little group of us left the chapel and set out to walk in silence from the convent, through the fields, down to the plum orchard out of sight and hearing of the convent, three fields away, enclosed and completely alone, carrying Scripture, incense and holy water.

There were Brother Anselm, Mother Gillian Mary, and Fr James Coutts representing Fr Donald Allchin my spiritual director. I have known James for thirty years, since we both had pastoral charges in Cardiff. He has followed my journey through the years, being more persuaded than I in the early days that this was the direction in which I would go.

It was a strange and moving procession, for as we walked I felt as if I was going to my death, and half-way down James took my arm for the rest of the way. I had a session with James some months later and he said that he had felt the same.

God may call you to such a "little death". He may lay his hand upon a cherished part of your life which must be yielded up so that out of that death something solid and eternal may emerge. Looked at negatively, such an act of surrender seems frightening, but if with St Francis we can name it "Sister Death" then it will become a dying-rising experience which manifests the gospel pattern. This was the pattern by which the apostle Paul lived (Galatians 2:20) and is the basic principle which Jesus embodied. "Unless a grain of wheat falls to the ground and dies, it remains only a single seed. But if it dies, it produces many seeds" (John 12:24).

When we got to the orchard entrance we said Psalm 121 and then did a "Jericho march" around the inside perimeter of the orchard saying Psalm 122. At the caravan entrance prayers of exorcism of dark powers and of protection and guidance were said.

James made a huge sign of the cross over me from head to toe, then looked at me and said: "for special protection". He certainly believes that anyone who travels this way will soon be up against darkness and attack.

We had agreed that I would not write for publication

17

during the first year, but I did keep a diary/spiritual journal, and looking at the entry for 2nd September, I read:

> Over the last few days I have lain low and feel something like a death has taken place and is still taking place in me. I am only now realizing that I have cut myself off from all my friends and am in a very precarious psychological state. And for the first time I wonder if I will be able to make it through the first year . . . I look forward to seeing Fr Donald on 23rd September.

Response

* Do you feel part of the same Church of Christ which contains within its tradition hermits and solitaries?

* Do you remember in prayer and action those who have been forcibly incarcerated and ill-treated for their faith and witness, as part of the same body?

* Perhaps you ought not only to read the story of the Desert Fathers and the eremitical tradition, but keep abreast of the suffering Church throughout the world. For we are one body.

Who follows Christ's insistent call
Must give himself, his life, his all,
Without one backward look.
Who puts his hand upon the plough
And glances back with anxious brow
His calling has mistook.
Christ claims him wholly for his own,
He must be Christ's and Christ's alone.

JOHN OXENHAM

18

DAY FOUR

Planning

SCRIPTURE: Hebrews 12:1–11. The race that lies before us

Prayer

Abba, Father:
It is with such a cry that I come to you. My feet are upon
the way and I am afraid, but I trust in you.
Although I feel alone my eyes are upon the Lord Jesus and
I am surrounded by a great cloud of witnesses who have
travelled this way before me.
Lead me on then, my Father; discipline me gently and let
my feet not stray from the path of your loving will;
Through Jesus Christ my Lord. Amen.

Reflection

You must not think, when you take this new direction into
God's unfolding will, that he will make all your decisions
and take all initiative from you. It is your mind and your
heart through which his will is to be expressed. Let me share
with you how it was with me.

Left to myself after the others had returned to the convent
and their own lives, I realized that at last the Lord had got
me here. I had been convinced over a number of years that
I was to come to a real trial of the solitary life, sharing in
some form of the eremitical (hermit) tradition. So I began
to let go my various ministries.

First of all I took on no more mission engagements, then was allowed not to be elected on to the brothers' Chapter of the Society of St Francis. I declined further invitations to retreats, lectures, prayer schools and preaching engagements and conferences.

Over the last year I made it clear to friends that I would be withdrawing from all the responsibilities with novices and professed brothers, closing my diary and reducing my correspondence to almost nil. Also I contacted all those for whom I had pastoral care in spiritual direction from various denominational backgrounds and pointed them elsewhere.

About a year before leaving Glasshampton I felt the Lord saying: "Be silent, or I shall silence you." This was not a threat but a loving promise − but I had to take it seriously. All this apparently negative letting go had to take place before I could realize the positive and life-giving way that is now before me.

I was stepping out not knowing where it would all lead. I had worked out a rather complicated plan of writing to about two hundred or so people who were anxious to support me. There was to be a tear-off part to the letter for those who would covenant to spend an agreed period of prayer each week, and their names would be kept on a list for future prayer letters sent out by one of the friars or a friend. But more and more I was reduced to simplicity in every way, and the letter I sent out eventually in August 1990 ran like this:

Dear . . . .
I had planned and worked out a longer and more involved letter, but I've come to see that the simpler the transition and the fewer the words the closer it will be to the will of God. There are just five things:

1 I want to express my deep gratitude to all who support me in prayer and have been patient because I have been unable to answer my backlog of correspondence.

2 I shall be moving out from Glasshampton mid-August and at the end of the month shall settle into the enclosure on the grounds of the Society of the Sacred Cross at Tymawr, with the kind permission and blessing of the Mother and sisters.

3 You will accept this lovingly and gently I know – but I shall not welcome *any* visits. It would embarrass the sisters and myself to have to say a gentle but firm "no".

4 Mail must not be sent to Tymawr. I do not expect to answer letters anyway, but requests for prayer can be sent c/o Brother Amos SSF at Glasshampton. I will still be attached to this house.

5 All my plans about prayer-partners and news-letters have folded up because of my present need to be aware and simple.

None of this indicates a withdrawal from love and sharing, but does indicate the need to be less fussy. This letter says enough and not too much, and I'm sure you will understand.

The fact that you receive this letter means that you are in my prayers each *Sunday morning*. I hope I may be in yours.

At the end of the first year I shall meet with my director/s and we shall listen to what the Lord is saying to us for the future.

In His love and care,
Ramon SSF

You can imagine the time and energy it took to see those who came to visit me and assure me of prayerful support,

and the letters – many of which never had a reply apart
from the "round-robin" reproduced above. It became so
difficult as the time drew nearer that I had to gently decline
people's requests to come to the monastery, especially as
some people now treated it so seriously as "the real thing".
I don't mean to make light of it, but after all we are *all* on
the Lord's path and I was only doing it a bit differently.
Looking back from this vantage point today I see that
perhaps they were more right than I thought.

Response

* Granted that our particular stories may be different, do
  you recognize that the path you walk is God's loving way
  for you?

* If you do not already have a counsellor or soul-friend,
  perhaps it is time you asked the Lord to lead you to someone with whom you can share your spiritual pilgrimage.

* Write into your journal a possible letter to such a person
  describing the kind of character you are and the kind of
  help you may need.

The Call

My friend, beware of me
Lest I should do
The very thing I'd sooner die than do,
In some way crucify the Christ in you.

If you are called to some great sacrifice,
And I should come to you with frightened eyes
And cry, "Take care, take care, be wise, be wise!"
See through my softness, then a fiend's attack,
And bid me get straight behind your back;

Planning

To your own conscience and your God be true
Lest I play Satan to the Christ in you.
And I would humbly ask of you in turn
That if some day in me Love's fires should burn
To whiteness, and a Voice should call
Bidding me leave my little for God's all,
If need be, you would thrust me from your side —
So keep love loyal to the Crucified.

FATHER ANDREW SDC

DAY FIVE

Settling

SCRIPTURE: 2 Kings 6:1–7. Building the prophets' dwelling

Prayer

My heavenly Father:
I realize that in this world I have no permanent dwelling,
and that I pitch my tent each day nearer heaven. Help me
in the practical necessities of each day, and in the energies
expended in daily work and play, to know your divine
stillness and to be centred upon your loving will, so that
in all things your love may overflow to other lives;
Through Jesus Christ my Lord. Amen.

Reflection

We all need space – a place on which to stand which is ours. This is true in a corporate as well as a personal sense. Even in a warm, responsive and secure family each member should be able to find the personal space and freedom to simply be themselves.

Over the last years of "upward mobility" obsession it has also paradoxically been distressing to find so many people unable to keep up mortgage payments, resulting in a repossessing of their homes. Two of our friars spent some time actually living among cardboard boxes in London, gaining a particular perspective on homelessness in an upwardly mobile society.

We all need *some* space, and even in the days of Elijah's

company of prophets in our reading, they felt cramped and constricted and took to building their own huts as they expanded in numbers. Like them we need space for reflection, self-discovery and prophecy. Such space enables us to experiment with lifestyle, to discover the dimension of prayer, allowing us to become more relaxed with ourselves and open to God and to our fellows.

I had wanted a small hut in which to explore the hermit life but I realized that until I was more permanently placed, a caravan might be more useful. So one day Mervyn rang the monastery and said: "Linda has seen a caravan advertised in the local rag," and he passed on the telephone number.

Next day Amos, Mervyn and I went to Stourport and met a delightful Irish Methodist couple who were selling their three-berth caravan, and when they knew why I wanted it, sold it for £350. Within a week three couples had paid for it, Molly made curtains for it, Michael carpentered a work-top, Peggy sewed ten foam cushions and Peter water-proofed the awning (more of that ill-fated awning later).

So by the end of August, after the service and blessing I was *in situ*.

I had a lot of experience of various timetables, and changes had to take place with changing seasons and hours of light and darkness, but to begin with it went like this:

4.00 a.m.	Rise
4.30 a.m.	Jesus Prayer and meditation
5.45 a.m.	Up to convent (while community was at prayer, etc.) for cleaning, painting; feeding hens and cleaning henhouses; various gardening/wood-chopping, etc.
7.30 a.m.	Back to caravan, ablutions, breakfast
8.30 a.m.	SSF morning prayer and meditation
9.30 a.m.	Study/reading/writing during morning

12.30 p.m.	SSF midday prayer
1.00 p.m.	Preparation and consumption of main meal
2.30 p.m.	Afternoon work: e.g. bookbinding/prayer-stool making/icon mounting; occasional painting exterior huts in grounds; forestry walking or jogging
5.30 p.m.	Light tea
6.00 p.m.	SSF evening prayer and meditation
7.00 p.m.	Secular reading (biographies, novels, etc.), listening to music
8.00 p.m.	Compline and bed

On Sundays I got up at 6.00 a.m. to do the hens, the rest of the morning being devoted to celebration of the eucharist and intercessions for all friends and those who asked for prayer. In the afternoon I listened to the radio and/or went walking/cycling (quiet country roads).

At first the weather was fine and then there were increasing downpours of rain and the fanlight developed a leak which I sealed with mastic. The small gas-cooker worked well with its two rings, grill and oven for bread.

I had spent the 1983/4 winter on the Lleyn Peninsula without heat and I planned to do the same here. It is good to have a 15kg. butane gas cylinder which lasts two to three months just for cooking.

For light I have the beautiful two-wick paraffin lamp which Molly and Michael gave me, though I shall not have to use it much until the darker nights. I made room in my timetable for weekly bread-making, washing of clothes, digging the loo in neighbouring fields and various other jobs.

So with a watertight caravan, warm clothes and the ability to cook food I hear St Paul's words: "We brought nothing into the world, and we cannot take anything out of the world; but if we have food and clothing, with these we shall be content" (1 Timothy 6:7f. RSV)

The interior of the caravan (just 12 × 6 feet) looked like this:

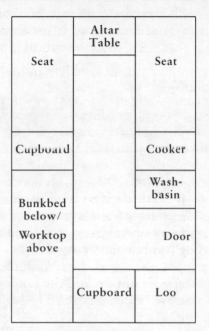

Seat	Altar Table	Seat
Cupboard		Cooker
		Wash-basin
Bunkbed below/ Worktop above		Door
	Cupboard	Loo

Caravan Hermitage

Response

* Review your life (within the context of your singleness or family) and make a note of the superfluous baggage you've accumulated over the years.

* Make a list of things you could/should get rid of (e.g., clothes, furniture, luxury equipment) and of organizations/people who would be grateful for gifts of such items. Consider making the gifts.

* Do it!

27

Father,
I abandon myself into your hands;
Do with me what you will.
Whatever you may do, I thank you:
I am ready for all, I accept all.

Let only your will be done in me,
    and in all your creatures.
I wish no more than this, O Lord.

Into your hands I commend my spirit;
I offer it to you
With all the love of my heart,
For I love you, O Lord,
And so need to give myself,
To surrender myself into your hands,
Without reserve,
And with boundless confidence,

For you are my Father.

PERE CHARLES DE FOUCAULD

28

DAY SIX

Freezing

SCRIPTURE: Psalm 147. The waters harden at his frost

Prayer

O God of nature and of grace:
In your hand is the changing of the year, the cycle of the
seasons, the stability of life within the circling year;
I give thanks that I meet you in the springtime of hope and
in the summer of joy, and that I feel your presence in the
melancholy of autumn and the chilling of winter;
Let me prove your faithfulness in all the changes and chances
of life and walk with you at last into the summerland of love;
Through Jesus Christ my Lord. Amen.

Reflection

The first two months of solitude, September and October, filled the whole valley with the glorious colour and texture of autumn. On my Sunday walks through the woodlands the rain and dew would be shimmering on the leaves in the morning or afternoon sun, and from the woodland ridge about a mile opposite my hermitage, further up the hillside, I could see my white caravan nestling in the fields behind the hedge.

But the days of November were wet, misty and cold, and ice soon began to appear. On Sundays the canticle at morning prayer is the *Benedicite*, containing the words:

Bless the Lord all winds that blow . . .
Bless the Lord dews and falling snows . . .
Bless the Lord frost and cold,
Bless the Lord you ice and snow;
Sing his praise and exalt him for ever.

It's one thing to sing the *Benedicite* to the plainsong tone 1, ending 2, but quite another to have to break the ice of the containers to give the hens fresh water and find a tap that isn't frozen.

Yet cold hands can be remedied more easily than a cold heart, and it is possible to do something about a frozen tap, but what about when we are frozen in fear, when we are paralysed stiff because of some psychological quirk of character or some secret sin or corrupting relationship in which we are entangled? The "frozen" metaphor is one which should enable us to examine our sluggish condition and cry to the Lord to thaw and warm our frozen hearts by the fire of the Holy Spirit:

O Thou who camest from above
the pure celestial fire to impart,
kindle a flame of sacred love
on the mean altar of my heart.

I said that I had a butane (blue) gas cylinder inside the caravan – inside because I had heard that butane can freeze in the winter. And it did! One morning in December at 4.15 a.m. I found that the water inside the caravan was frozen and so was the butane gas – it was ten degrees below freezing. Later that day I managed to fix up a propane (orange) cylinder, and lo and behold, the gas ring lit up. What a welcome moment – I boiled the kettle thankfully.

On Christmas Eve it was wonderful to be alone to welcome the advent of our Saviour, and it was with joy that I lit my candles and celebrated the midnight mass – alone yet in the company of the Society of the Sacred Cross here and of the Society of St Francis and the people of God throughout the world.

All went well and I tucked myself up with praise and gratitude at about 1.45 a.m., and shortly afterwards the wind rose and torrents of rain beat upon the caravan roof, and the canvas awning on the front began to billow, shake and groan. It had been shrinking in the cold weather and I had experienced increasing difficulty in zipping the door flap. Then as the wind rose to 70 m.p.h. and 80 m.p.h., rushing down the opposite hillside and up the hill towards me, I heard two of the poles collapse.

So at about 3.00 a.m. there was I in my pyjamas, battling with the elements, trying to put the aluminium poles together again in the darkness, while knocking in the tent-pins with the mallet. On Christmas day, before I had my beans on toast, I collected some very large stones, as heavy as I could manage, and covered the tent-pins and lower flap of the awning.

All to no avail. The awning went on billowing for a week and on New Year's night I gave up the struggle gracefully and from my bunk bed I said out loud: "Oh, let it go . . ." – and it went! Collapsed beyond recall.

I was reduced in space with no storage outside the caravan and I learned a great deal, not only about this episode being a parable of my life, reduced and simplified more and more, but also about the storms that will one day cause the tent of my earthly existence to collapse. That is only one side of the truth, "for we know that when this tent we live in – our body here on earth – is torn down, God will have a house in heaven for us to live in, a home he himself has made, which will last for ever" (2 Corinthians 5:1 GNB). What a wonderful hope and assurance to read that passage to verse 10 and its glorious conclusion of appearing before the Lord clothed with our heavenly body.

"For ever with the Lord!"
Amen, so let it be!
Life from the dead is in that word,
'Tis immortality.
Here in the body pent,
Absent from him I roam,
Yet nightly pitch my moving tent
A day's march nearer home.

Response

* Link the four seasons in your journal with words which may convey the pattern of changing seasons in your life – e.g., spring = birth; summer = growth; autumn = maturity; winter = death.

* Associate these themes with a meditation on flux and mutability, and your ability to adapt to changing circumstances in your own experience.

* Let this lead to a reflection on the stability of God's love in the midst of life's changing seasons.

The Cycle of Love

God has ordered the natural cycle of seasons according to a pattern of variety and change, design and fruitfulness. So we find reflected in our inner lives a seasonal and spiritual cycle which promotes our good and God's glory. Springtime captures all those moments of new life and hope which burst forth in our soul – the rising of the sap, the putting forth of buds and blossom, the anticipation of beauty and wonder. Summer encapsulates the full glory of awakened energies, the fulfilment of early hopes and longings and the long days of joyful labour and happy relationships.

Autumn pictures the ripening and gathering of maturing

fruitfulness, the maturity of wise counsel and experience, and the joyfulness of work well done. Winter brings the cold blasts of declining days, the falling of the sap and the acceptance of a good and gentle death.

Yet for the believer, even in the freezing winter season the bright shoots of spring are already stirring in the deep soil of the soul. The changing of the seasons is the rhythmic movement of God's Spirit in the earth, reflected in the body, mind and spirit of our human life.

DAY SEVEN

Cleaning

SCRIPTURE: John 13:1–17. Jesus washes the disciples' feet

Prayer

Lord Jesus Christ:
You submitted yourself to the waters of the Jordan though
*   without sin,*
and knelt to wash the soiled feet of your disciples;
Wash us inwardly from the impurities of secret lusts, and
*   outwardly from the daily acts of selfishness and pride;*
Through the cleansing merits of your precious blood. Amen.

Reflection

It is strange that though Buddhist, Hindu, Muslim and Jewish devotees have clear rules and counsels about diet, cleanliness, physical exercises and hygiene, many Christians feel there is something either distasteful or irrelevant about such areas. Yet water baptism is the initiatory rite of the Christian faith and the washing of the feet is the most telling symbol of cleansing and humility. Jesus made these outward and external signs channels of inward and spiritual grace just as he took the common symbols of bread and wine and gave us his precious body and blood.

But he did not stay with the external sign. He ignored legalistic cleansing rituals like the washing of hands or the cleansing of vessels so that attention could be given to inward cleansing and renewal. As he said: "Out of the heart come evil thoughts, murder, adultery, sexual immorality, theft, false testimony, slander. These are what make a man unclean; but eating with unwashed hands does not make him unclean" (Matthew 15:19, 20 RSV).

"Cleanliness is next to godliness", quoted my mother fervently when she led me to the bath as a small boy, and she was certain those words came from holy Scripture. She also urged a regular change of underwear "in case you get run over", and a combing of my hair before going to bed "in case you die in the night". I couldn't quite follow the latter, and I wondered what she would think of some of the Old Testament prophets or Desert Fathers who were flea-ridden or of the "Spiritual" Franciscan friars who never washed their habits.

If I was to get run over on one of my hitching adventures it would be quite possible for me to be wearing my colourful, jazzy "Flintstone" boxer shorts and the T-shirt with its very doubtful logo unfit for Christian eyes. Combined with a Franciscan habit they would raise some eyebrows in the casualty department, though they would be clean!

These matters of cleanliness and hygiene are a basic part of my life in solitude, for unlike living in family or community, living alone places particular responsibility upon me to be diligent, for neglect in these areas soon makes itself felt!

At the end of my first year in solitude I had some days with my sister and friends in Swansea and my first bath for a year! In the hermitage, with no bathing/shower facilities you must make sure you keep clean. Regular changes of clothes and bed linen, regular cleaning of hut or caravan and leaving no dishes unwashed – all these things are important. No flush toilet means an Elsan and every Saturday morning I dig a hole in the neighbouring field and renew the loo. It is estimated that we in Britain use up to

150 gallons of water per head every week – baths and toilet flushing accounting for much of that. I use about ten gallons a week, my ablution water becoming my washing-up water and then being used for my loo.

The washing and drying of clothes can be a headache (no ironing, of course), but I do have access to a weekly hot-water tap and that is a great help. At the beginning I had the offer of convent facilities for these things but it seemed to me that if simplicity was my style, then to have "use" of baths, washing machine and fridge while living "simply" in a field would be daft.

I sometimes think about the simplicity of John the Baptist and the desert monks in their ascetic life and freedom from care about clothes, cleanliness and diet. Simply locust beans and wild honey to eat, a garment of camel hair and shelter in a cave above the Jordan. Climate must dictate differences – recently during my early morning meditation I was wearing six layers of clothing, plus a balaclava and a blanket wrapped around me. There were the mitigating circumstances of being surrounded, on my prayer stool, by three windows thick with ice and the water inside being frozen. I have not yet attained the charism of melting the snow and ice by my spiritual fervour while wearing a single cotton covering like some of the Himalayan ascetics!

Creatures of the natural order teach me about cleanliness too. Over the last two weeks three baby rabbits have been feeding and playing beneath my window. I've called them Abraham, Isaac and Jacob – though they could equally be Sarah, Rebekah and Rachel! This morning Abraham has been washing and cleaning himself, contented and relaxed in this enclosure of safety.

Perhaps my mother was right after all – the measure of discipline and cleanliness is the measure of sanity and maturity – and therefore of spirituality.

Jesus gets to the root of the matter. It's not a thing of rules and regulations, of ritual religious practices and liturgical lip-service, but of a pure heart, a transformed life and a compassionate spirit. When he laid aside his outer garment and knelt before his disciples to wash their feet he embodied the dual message of cleanliness and humility. Cleanliness of body and mind results from a pure heart. And if we get our priorities right the rest will follow.

Response

* Are you sometimes more concerned with outward appearance and a good image than with the inner realities of truth and holiness?

* If on Maundy Thursday you were asked to participate in a service of foot-washing, write down what your response would be.

* If a wayfarer who had been sleeping rough presented himself at your door late one evening (presuming you had a spare bed), asking for food, a bath and a night's shelter, write down what you would do.

Outward and Inward Cleansing

The leprosy patient said: "I want you to wash me all over, because I smell so bad that I cannot stand it myself."

Then St Francis immediately had water boiled with many sweet-scented herbs. Next, he undressed the man with leprosy and began to wash him . . . while another friar poured the water over him.

And by a divine miracle, wherever St Francis touched him with his holy hands, the leprosy disappeared, and the flesh remained completely healed. And as externally the water washed his body and the flesh began to heal and be wholly cleansed from leprosy, so too interiorly his soul began to be healed and cleansed. And when the man with leprosy saw himself being healed externally, he immediately began to have great compunction and remorse for his sins. And he began to cry very bitterly. Just as his body was washed with water and cleansed from leprosy, so his conscience was baptized by tears and contrition and cleansed from all evil and sin.

The Little Flowers of St Francis

DAY EIGHT

Working

SCRIPTURE: Exodus 31:1–11. Artisans anointed by the Spirit

Prayer

O Christ the Master Carpenter of Nazareth,
Who at the last, through wood and nails, purchased our
*   whole salvation,*
Wield well your tools in the workshop of your world,
So that we who come rough-hewn to your bench may here be
*   fashioned to a truer beauty of your hand;*
For your own name's sake. Amen.

Reflection

It was not an accident that Jesus was considered an artisan and that manual work was honoured in the tradition in which he was brought up. "Isn't this the carpenter? Isn't this Mary's son?" (Mark 6:3). The people may have been surprised that a carpenter taught with such wisdom and did such mighty works, but the tradition claimed that the skill and craftsmanship of the artisan was a gift of the Holy Spirit.

I often felt that I had four thumbs in our carpentry work at school, and so it has been a great joy for me to develop a skill in making prayer-stools for so many people, and now working on a simple scheme for a book-rest soon to go into production. Together with icon-mounting and bookbinding I have quite a workshop going some afternoons, the proceeds of which go to Glasshampton, and in turn I am provided with gas and basic foodstuffs.

But it is not the financial support that is important but the creative dimension in manual work. After all, the desert hermits used to plait mats and baskets, and though they did have an outlet for them the *fact* of manual work was the primary thing. If necessary they would plait for hours and then undo the work and start again, while bringing manual work and prayer together.

In repetitive manual work it is a skill of balance and harmony to bring it into the rhythm of the Jesus Prayer (see p. 48f). But having said that, I do not use this time for more general intercession, because much manual work deserves the kind of concentration in relaxation which is called *mindfulness* (see my *Heaven on Earth*, pp. 28ff.). Mindfulness is the giving of myself completely to one thing, with such gentle concentration that I become lost in the joy and creativity of the work in hand. Speaking of Bezalel, the creative artisan with his vocation to work in the tabernacle, we read: "I have filled him with the Spirit of God, with skill, ability and knowledge in all kinds of crafts – to make artistic designs for work in gold, silver and bronze, to cut and set stones, to work in wood, and to engage in all kinds of craftsmanship" (Exodus 31:3–5).

I have been reading a delightful book, *Trigger in Europe* by William Holt who, with his ex-rag-and-bone horse Trigger, travelled 20,000 miles throughout Europe, sleeping in the open air together. Bill was sixty-seven years old when he began this adventure and it was financed simply and wholly by his sketching and painting along the way. He had with him his charcoal, oil paints, brushes and cartridge paper and he produced charcoal sketches of scenes and people which were quickly bought. The book depicts the blending together of relationships, creativity and simple lifestyle that attracts me greatly. Bill writes:

In Paris I accumulated quite a fund, sketching on the banks of the Seine, or in the early morning around Les Halles painting the colourful scenes in the fruit and vegetable markets, my pictures selling on sight. My charcoal sketches of the bridges over the Seine were popular though my impressions of the gargoyles of Notre Dame appealed to fewer, but fetched higher prices. Over the Rue d'Arcole the towers of Notre Dame seemed to separate and suddenly a row of gargoyles leapt out at you, long necks craning, jaws open, ears well back, and looking down into the Rue du Cloître, beasts and demons crane their necks, howling. They sit out horizontally without falling down as if the cathedral was the centre of gravity.

I appreciate and envy this ability to carry within oneself the possibility of art and earning one's keep in the same act of creation. I have often envied buskers who were accomplished musicians, like the fellow who played jazz on a saxophone outside the Festival Hall, or the young man who played the flute superbly when I last visited Exeter, near the cathedral. If such busking could combine an act of creative integrity and communication together with the receiving of money as a token of appreciation, this would be what I would be aiming at.

Perhaps that is why I used to feel such joy in fellowship with Mark in his frequent visits to Glasshampton monastery. He is a furniture designer/maker and manifests that very integrity in creative manual work of which we have been speaking. It is no accident that he used to play and sing some post-communion music on his guitar at our Sunday eucharist. In a recent letter to me about contemplative prayer he wrote: "My work is largely solitary and allows expanses of time in which to be guided in prayer and contemplation and simple enjoyment of God in creativity. I sometimes feel He really enjoys my work and delights in my expressions."

One of our SSF brothers has a great devotion to manual work in the garden and to natural beauty, and I remember the great delight we shared when he showed me a garden of prayer that he had established for a community in the south of England. I wrote to him expressing something of my endeavour to "get things together", and it indicates how I was feeling during my first year:

> You are in mind during this period as I go to the convent at about 6.15 a.m. and clean/feed/water the thirty-six chickens and do digging/mulching/weeding/chopping wood/painting and decorating, etc. when there is no one about. The community is at terce/mass/breakfast/conference until about 8.15 a.m.
>
> One morning before sunrise I was digging in the vegetable garden, blowing steamy breath into the cold air, and then the sun showed its face and rose in great glory, in pinks and blues and greys and whites and all tints between, and I began to sing:

> Still, still with Thee, when purple morning breaketh,
> When the bird waketh, and the shadows flee;
> Fairer than morning, lovelier than the daylight
> Dawns the sweet consciousness – I am with Thee.

But lest we get caught up in a spirituality which is not earthed, this is the place to remember words from the Rule of St Benedict in which it says of the monk's care of material things: "He will regard all utensils and goods of the monastery as sacred vessels of the altar." It is in the concrete reality of daily life that God is to be found, and especially in the sweat and grime of manual work well done.

But while I am painting and digging and chopping wood and bookbinding in the joyful awareness of God in the middle of the country, what about the grinding, repetitive work which for many men and women empties life of its meaning, or the lack of work which makes many people feel redundant in soul?

I have no wage or salary, but my community maintains me, and I need not depend on the work I do to keep body and soul together. This frees me from financial or psychological anxiety, and I have no family to support or hire-purchase or mortgage payments to make. My caravan is in no danger of repossession.

Of course I could, by next year, be back in an urban community house, working four nights a week as an SRN in a geriatric hospital and be spending days and weekends in parish work and counselling.

But as it is, I am here, taking into my thinking, praying and writing some of the economic, social and political burdens and problems of our time. It seems to me that the Franciscan life with its simplicity and discipline, and the involvement of brothers and sisters in various religions, social and caring responsibilities, is a pattern for our country at present.

Houses are still being repossessed, various grades of homelessness are before our eyes, unemployment continues to be a scourge, caring agencies are financially pressed and we persist in immense military expenditure.

My vocation is a small part of the wider Franciscan life, and the positive value and blessing of work is one part of that pattern which imparts joy to human life.

Response

* Note the importance of the context in which Jesus lived his earthly life as a) a manual worker; b) a wayside preacher; c) a man of wisdom and compassion.

* Do you recognize the creative springs of vitality in mental or manual work, so that any kind of work which furthers

creativity and compassion may be an expression of the dynamic of the Holy Spirit?

* Have you established an harmonious balance of the mental and the physical in your lifestyle? If you are sedentary, write down possible manual work and exercise you could incorporate into your life. If you are a manual worker, write down some learning tasks in which your mind could be stretched. Seek advice if necessary.

Mindfulness. I have come to love and treasure this word, for it is one of those "uniting" words which indicate a simple human practice found in all contemplative human beings, though they may not know the word. It means the ability to give oneself wholly to one thing, to one person, to one discipline, and to allow oneself to be caught or taken up into an absorbing pattern of meaning . . . The words *Distraction, dislocation, preoccupation*, indicate unmindful inattention to the work in hand or to the person who needs your undivided attention.

To chop an onion, peel a turnip, grate a carrot or scrub a potato can be a great joy. And if done in mindfulness it can be an act of meditation and a source of tranquillity and thankfulness.

Heaven on Earth

DAY NINE

Sleeping

SCRIPTURE: Acts 12:1–16. Peter sleeping without fear

Prayer

Be present, O merciful God, and protect us through the hours of this night, so that we who are wearied by the changes and chances of this life may rest in your eternal changelessness;
Through Jesus Christ our Lord. Amen.

Reflection

I always enjoy introducing new people to Compline or Night Prayer. It is the monastic office which is said or sung before going to sleep. If visitors to a friary, guests, wayfarers, campers or non-Christians stay away from other services in the chapel they will usually come to Compline. Why? Because it is brief and simple; because it is the end of the day; because it is not threatening; but more than all, because it is full of assurance and safety, promising the care and protection of God through the dark and silent hours of the night.

Interwoven throughout the Scripture, psalms, hymns and prayers is the sense of the undergirding, sustaining and healing power of God renewing our bodies and spirits and protecting us from evil and the powers of darkness.

It can be a very moving experience to sing Compline in the candlelit chapel of one of our friaries, around the campers' bonfire on the last night, in the intimate circle of home and family or around the bed of a sick loved one who is too ill to recite or sing but who knows the familiar words.

It is important for me to be able to move gently from Compline into sleep and one of the joys of solitude at the end of the day is to begin Compline with the words: "The Lord Almighty grant us a quiet night and a perfect end," and before the blessing to say: "In peace we will lie down and sleep; For you alone, Lord, make us dwell in safety."

The gift of sleep is one of the Lord's greatest blessings, as those who suffer from any form of insomnia know. So many people are kept awake by pain, loneliness, worry, drugs, fear, stress or sheer exhaustion. And there are those who are wakeful because of a sense of guilt and conscience over evil committed or planned, or even because of hatred or lack of forgiveness nurtured over the years and resulting in an inability to rest in peace.

Of course, the gift of sleep is not incompatible with being wakened by the Lord for times of intercession or adoration. It may be that you are sleeping one night and suddenly you are awakened by the Lord because he wants to communicate some message or experience to you. Perhaps he simply wants to remind you that he loves you, or wants to warn you, and this is the best time to do it. Or perhaps a loved one is in pain or need and you are awakened to intercede for her, giving strength and hope as it is needed.

Night periods spent in meditation or prayer are often qualitatively richer than day periods because darkness can deepen concentration with no likelihood of disturbance. Sleep after such a period may be even more conducive to deep rest.

It may be that sleep is impossible because the threatening storms and trials of life make you feel like the disciples on the Lake of Galilee when threatened by the wild elements (Mark 4:35–41):

> Fierce raged the tempest o'er the deep,
> Watch did your anxious servants keep,
> But you were wrapped in guileless sleep,
> Calm and still.

Jesus was asleep! The wind and waves threatened to engulf the boat and drown the terrified disciples. How can he sleep when the anxieties, pains and problems of an uncertain existence buffet and frighten us?

Perhaps it is only then that we realize that Jesus is asleep within the boat of our soul and we awaken him within us and call upon him: "Jesus, I am sinking. Do you not care?"

If our heart goes out to him in a cry for salvation he will hear us and command the wild elements and powers that threaten our sinking soul: "Peace! Be still!" And we shall find rest and peace.

Then there are times when we need to sleep and are unable, maybe because we are overtired or anxious. I'm not speaking now of chronic insomnia, for that needs specialist medical treatment, but of difficulty in relaxing and letting go all the tension and frenetic activity of days of harassment and worry — we just can't unwind. I'm not now going to recommend a contemplative technique as a soporific aid to sleep, but one of the by-products of mastering a simple technique is that it enables you to relax and helps you towards necessary sleep.

If you are lying awake, a simple repetitive prayer like the Jesus Prayer can deepen your intimate communication with God, and in turn this may lead you into restful sleep. Something like this:

You are in bed preparing to sleep. Lie upon your back with your arms at your sides, palms upwards. Quietly talk each part of your body from your head to your feet into a gentle and easy relaxation by stretching and relaxing. For instance: "Head and neck muscles — stretch and relax

48

. . . stretch and relax;" "Shoulders and upper arms – stretch and relax . . . stretch and relax." And so on, right down to your toes.

Then, when your whole body is relaxed, give your attention to breathing, from your abdomen instead of from the top of your chest – what is called belly breathing. There is no strain or stress in any of this – your body is relaxed and your breathing gentle. Then lift your heart to God and begin to say the Jesus Prayer:

> Lord Jesus Christ/Son of God
> Have mercy on me/a sinner

You can begin the prayer audibly and then continue it mentally, and it can be repeated rhythmically according to your inward and outward breathing or with your heartbeat.

Take your time over all this or it will prove to be counter-productive and keep you awake. But if your body is relaxed and your breathing easy as you repeat the prayer, then after ten or fifteen minutes you may find that you can change your position and give yourself to sleep.

I repeat that I am not advocating the Jesus Prayer as a sleeping technique, but how good it is to be able to go to sleep with the name of Jesus on your lips, in your mind and in your heart.

Some Christians deprive themselves of sleep occasionally or on a regular basis in order to keep vigil for the sleepless and the suffering of the world. Many contemplative Orders think of their night office in this way, and this is a conscious and voluntary discipline for the sake of others.

Then there are many people who, though they are not chronic insomniacs, still have a problem with sleep yet use it positively and offer it to the Lord, as Etta Gullick reveals in one of her prayers:

O Lord, let me sleep! You have said that you will give your beloved sleep. I know you love me, please give me sleep. Or let me rest quietly in you and realize that I am sharing with you the sleeplessness of the starving, the lonely, the lost and the old who are so much worse off than I. Let me know that my wakefulness is not wasted but helps to make up what is lacking in your suffering.

Sleep is a time when our physical and mental powers are renewed and it is also a time when God is at work in our spiritual lives (see Day Twenty-two on Dreaming). In the Eden story God created Eve from the rib of the sleeping Adam (Genesis 2:21). It was during sleep that the vision of Jacob's ladder communicated awe and wonder to Jacob (Genesis 28:10–22).

Peter was so relaxed and resting in God after his arrest that he went to sleep chained between two guards, and the angel had to strike him, shine upon him, give him sharp instructions and break his chains (Acts 12:1–17). It's a wonderful story and easy to see with what great delight Charles Wesley saw in it a dramatic picture of salvation:

> Long my imprisoned spirit lay
> Fast bound in sin and nature's night;
> Thine eye diffused a quickening ray,
> I woke, the dungeon flamed with light;
> My chains fell off, my heart was free;
> I rose, went forth, and followed Thee.

Of course, sleep can also be dangerous or frightening, like the time that Samson went to sleep in the arms of Delilah – there's no need for me to draw the moral from that story! (Judges 16:4–22). Or when Saul neglected his guard and went to sleep in open camp and David had opportunity to kill him (1 Sam. 26:1–12). Then there are such creepy nightmares as described in that evocative passage in Job 4:13–17.

Much of our sleep pattern is formed in childhood, and if love and security are part of the atmosphere there are fewer problems in later life. One of my night prayers was theologically suspect yet it gave me a warm sense of protection in the darkness:

> Matthew, Mark, Luke and John
> Bless the bed that I lie on;
> Four white angels round my bed
> To guard my tired and sleepy head.

Another of the prayers which should have made me uncomfortable but actually had the opposite effect of ultimate safety was:

> Now I lay me down to sleep
> I pray Thee, Lord, my soul to keep;
> And if I die before I wake
> I pray Thee, Lord, my soul to take.

People who do months or years on night duty imbibe quite a different perspective on life and their fellows, depending on the job they do. When I worked nights at Sully Chest Hospital on the south Glamorgan coast I remember nights when all was silent and the phases of the moon were reflected in the calm sea and all the patients were asleep. It was on such a night, when the world was sleeping, that I heard a clear and compulsive call to the ministry.

All these things are in my mind as this day moves towards its close in my hermitage, surrounded by fields running down to Whitebrook. The sun sets to the sound of bleating sheep and lambs and two, and then three, small rabbits nibble the greenery in my enclosure below my window.

So it is that I gather my whole day together, containing my work, prayer, study and writing, holding them with loved ones and friends in my heart as I move from Evensong to Compline and sleep. The God of Israel neither slumbers nor sleeps but protects and guards me through the hours of darkness until earth's evening gives way to the morning of eternity.

Response

* Do you consciously commend yourself and the world into the care and protection of God before you sleep?

* Do you recognize the gift of God in restorative sleep and are you grateful for the rhythm of your life through day and night?

* Why not obtain a copy of Compline and begin to say the night office alone or with your family/friends as a fitting end to the day?

Keep watch, dear Lord, with those who work, or watch, or weep this night, and give your angels charge over those who sleep. Tend the sick, Lord Christ; give rest to the weary, bless the dying, soothe the suffering, pity the afflicted, shield the joyous; and all for your love's sake. Amen.

ST AUGUSTINE

DAY TEN

Cooking

SCRIPTURE: Genesis 25:29–34. A birthright of red stew

Prayer

Lord Jesus Christ:
You are my food and drink, my medicine and health;
Grant that, feeding upon your holy word,
and sharing in the communion of your body and blood,
I may joyfully receive you, the Bread of Life,
and share this living bread with all who hunger;
For your dear name's sake. Amen.

Reflection

St Francis was a man of extremes in every way. One of the less edifying things he did was to forbid the soaking of beans and pulses overnight because that would have been preparing for the exigencies of the future, refusing to live a day at a time in taking thought for the morrow.

I am a Franciscan and try to live a day at a time in what many would think of as extreme simplicity, but I am not blind in my following of St Francis. He shames my hypocrisy and carnality most of the time, but sometimes he is more extreme than Jesus.

Anyway, I soak red kidney beans (or soya, black-eyed, mung, flageolet and haricot) overnight for the typical kind of main meal I prepare the next day. Jacob's "mess of pottage" couldn't be more sustaining than mine, though Esau despised and bartered away his birthright inheritance for a bowl of it. "Look, I am about to die," he said. "What good is the birthright to me?" He had a point, but that was certainly grasping the pleasure of the moment and losing the blessing of the future. What spiritual gain and loss in a bowl of stew!

Let me share my somewhat unorthodox version of Jacob's red pottage that I am preparing today. It is more primitive than some of the stylized recipes in my book *Heaven on Earth*.

Ingredients:

Small cupful of red kidney beans (soaked overnight)
1 medium onion
1 apple cut into wedges
Small wedges of carrot, swede, potato (or any available vegetables)
Some shredded cabbage
Teaspoon of dried (or fresh) herbs
2 tablespoons of olive (or vegetable) oil
2 tablespoons of wholemeal flour
2 tablespoons of soya sauce
1 vegetable cube (or Marmite)
1 small tin of chopped tomatoes (or fresh)
1 tablespoon of tomato puree
1 tablespoon of marmalade
Garlic salt to taste
½ pint of water

Method:

1 Pressure-cook beans for half an hour (cook enough to last four meals)
2 Into saucepan put oil, fruit and vegetables on low heat
3 After 10 minutes, add tomatoes, flour, soya, veg. cube, garlic salt and water
4 Bring close to boiling point, simmer 10–15 minutes
5 When both are ready, spoon a portion of Jacob's pottage over portion of beans. Repeat if hungry!

I have an infinite variety of such concoctions (sometimes curried) to combine with various beans, pulses, pasta, rice, TVP (textured vegetable protein) chunks/mince, sosmix, nutroast or hard-boiled eggs. I usually use a decent brand of vegetable oil, but at Christmas I received a bottle of "extra-virgin" olive oil from my editor. I wondered if she was communicating some hidden meaning!

I am not commending this recipe to others at this point, simply explaining what is a typical main meal for me. Apart from that, I would have a bowl of porridge in the morning, and sometimes a bread roll with honey, jam or marmalade in the evening.

This is a long way from the asceticism of living on a cabbage leaf like some of the fourth-century desert hermits in Egypt, Palestine, Arabia and Persia. But my goal is not to become a gaunt ascetic with rickets, but to serve God with a sane mind in a healthy body – *mens sana in corporo sano*, as the Latin tag has it.

Belonging to a community or family frees a person (save the cook) from concerns over diet and basic nutritional matters, but living alone heightens responsibility in this as well as other areas.

Again, I would neither mix ash nor cold water with my meals as St Francis did. Indeed I enjoy my bowl of hot porridge on a winter morning, with its spoonful of syrup. It makes me appreciate the central heating system of my own body as I face the wintry weather while using gas for cooking only.

There is a great deal of spirituality involved in the growing, preparing, cooking and eating of vegetables, so let me include one more recipe – but this time bread-making. My mini gas-cooker has two rings and does include a small oven, and that makes a weekly bake possible, consisting of eight bread rolls.

Ingredients:

1½ lbs wholemeal (or mixed) flour
1 sachet of dried yeast
1½ teaspoons of salt
1 tablespoon of honey or syrup
1 tablespoon of vegetable oil
1 pint of warm (almost hot) water

Method:

1 Mix flour, salt, yeast and oil in a bowl
2 Gradually stir in water/honey with a wooden spoon and
   mix to a pliable dough
3 Turn out on to a floured surface and knead for 10 minutes
4 Cut into eight pieces and form into rolls
5 Place on greased tin and put in oven to prove on low gas
6 When doubled in size (about 20 minutes) increase heat to
   high reg.
7 Bake for 20 minutes until brown – a hollow sound when
   tapped.

This is primitive, of course, because I have no warm place
for proving besides the oven itself, and no temperature levels
on the cooker. In any case, apart from basic amounts I am
intuitive about bread-making, and in two years of caravan
bread it has never refused to rise.

One day I ran out of flour and begged some by note from
the convent. Then I took one of the resulting rolls and put
it into my box in the tractor shed for Brother Brian. The
next morning I found a beautiful waterfall photograph with
a note on the back: "Thank you so much for sharing bread
in many ways. It was delicious and very special to both body
and soul. Truly bread of angels and a gift of grace, holy
communion! – Brian." I don't know if he realized that I
do use my own bread for the eucharist.

Response

* Consider St Paul's words: "Whether you eat or drink or whatever you do, do it all for the glory of God" (1 Corinthians 10:31).

* Write down some steps you can take to ensure greater simplicity and wholesomeness in diet, avoiding overindulgence.

* Go through your larder/freezer, deciding not to replenish unhealthy items but to incorporate basic healthy foods.

There is particular joy in growing vegetables, in gathering wholesome ingredients for the preparing and cooking of nutritious food, and in baking your own bread. Co-operation with the natural order and the gregarious sharing of meals around a common table with family and friends promotes human reciprocity and fellowship and gives glory to God.

If we can move towards better farming practices, less chemical and more organic, and if we can grow in the awareness that we are stewards of our planet and fellow-creatures with animals, then the roots of our being will be nourished and we shall eat and drink to the praise of God.

DAY ELEVEN

Replenishing

SCRIPTURE: Luke 12:13–34. The capitalist fool and the simple life

Prayer

O Merciful Creator:
Your hand is open to replenish the needs of every living
*   creature;*
Give us grateful hearts for the generosity of your gifts and
*   enable us in living simply to share our abundance and to*
*   seek the values and compassion of your Kingdom;*
Through Jesus Christ our Lord. Amen.

Reflection

I've been checking today. Checking my stores against my check list of needs and checking my life against Scripture and the Desert Father tradition. Our reading contains the parable of the rich fool whose harvest was so good that there was danger of a grain mountain. He could have distributed his harvest to the poor or sold it and given away the profit. Instead he decided to build bigger barns, store more capital, set himself up for many years, as he said to himself: "Take life easy; eat, drink and be merry."

Jesus was a good preacher, and as he told the story he put a sting into the tail, and the punch line goes: "But God said to him, 'You fool! This very night your soul will be demanded from you. Then who will get what you have prepared for yourself?' "

Then Jesus goes on to speak about not worrying about life, about food and drink or about the morrow. Seek the kingdom of God and leave the worrying and provision of material needs to him.

St Francis was such an extreme follower of Jesus that he went beyond such teaching, for he would not even allow the friars to soak beans for the next day! Jesus' band of disciples had a treasurer (even though it was Judas), but Francis did not allow himself or his friars even to *touch* money.

I'm supposed to be living a simple life but I have a cylinder of propane gas connected for cooking and one spare. My check list says: flour, pasta, dried milk, porridge oats, assorted beans, pulses, sosmix, TVP, margarine, baked beans, soup mix, coffee powder, marmalade; and under "luxuries" is written: peanut butter, honey, dried fruit.

I don't drink alcohol, smoke or eat meat, but compared with some of the desert dads who seemed to live on cabbage leaves, oil and salt, I feed sumptuously. I certainly seem to do planning for the morrow, for the monastery vehicle from Glasshampton brings supplies every four months or so, with wood, varnish, butt hinges, etc. for prayer stools and icon-mounting. But the Lord has a way of cutting me down to size as I described when my fancy awning blew away in the January storms and as happened yesterday when I developed a new leak in the roof.

Nevertheless the Lord is very gracious and he tempers the wind to the shorn lamb, for with every new demand he makes a gracious provision and enables me to see his disciplining grace in every sacrifice and his generosity in replenishing my supplies.

I'm glad I don't have to go out with my begging bowl as did the early friars. I can cut some cabbage from the vegetable patch as I did today and together with onions, potatoes, red beans and soya sauce I produce an adequate main meal. This is very bare and simple compared to the way some westerners eat, but sheer luxury in comparison with victims of drought, flood, famine, hunger or violence in much of the world. As Christians we may think we ought to be relatively poor but we cannot help but be relatively rich.

I'm not now preaching asceticism from my hermitage – I'll say a bit more about that under tomorrow's theme – and I'm not an ascetic anyway. I'm really reflecting upon the goodness of God and urging a grateful spirit.

I look at the shelf above my head and see the containers bearing the labels which proclaim the faithfulness of God. They are marked: Dried Milk, Rice, Black-eyed Beans, Split Peas, Lentils, Olive Oil (extra virgin!) and TVP (textured vegetable protein). When I pray "Give us this day our daily bread," I am always aware of praying it for the wider world but I also help to answer my own prayers, for every week I do a bake of eight bread rolls.

And what about mental and spiritual replenishment? As I have organized my food and work supplies, so I cater for mind and heart. Every week I receive the *Weekly Guardian* and the *Tablet*. These, together with occasional books, keep my mind active, providing fuel for thinking and praying about the Church and the world. The structure of my day provides definite times for liturgical prayer with a daily input of Scripture and the early morning for silent waiting upon God.

Of course there may be liturgical busyness without real prayer taking place, and the devil knows the Bible but it does not do him any good! Charles Wesley writes of "fresh supplies of love", for the spiritual replenishment of delight in God and a sense of his presence are gifts of the Holy Spirit. No amount of methodical organization substitutes for a receptive openness and longing for the fire of the Spirit. Therefore I constantly confess my need of God's grace and affirm that it is only by his initiative that I am replenished, renewed and made continually aware of the movement of the Holy Spirit within my daily experience.

Of course you can't store up spiritual supplies as I store up my beans and pulses for the next six months, or as a camel stores up water in its hump. We need new strength for each day and a fresh experience of God at each step of the way. There are no spiritual capitalists. But there are the kind of spiritual reserves that are built up in the daily disciplines of trust and prayer. When we pray for a good death and exercise compassion and forgiveness in our relationships we are building a healthy resistance to evil and an openness to God's continual grace. We cannot expect to be immune from danger in conflict if we neglect attention to the armour of God in times of peace.

But now it's raining again and I have neglected to repair the leak in my roof.

Response

* As you replenish your food stocks for the coming week, keep the word "simplicity" before you.

* If as a result there is a radical difference in the cost, it is time to do some stocktaking on your lifestyle.

* Use this as an analogy for your spiritual life. How do you replenish supplies of compassion, patience, gentleness, perseverence?

Once some robbers came to the monastery and said to one of the elders: We have come to take away everything that is in your cell. And he said: My sons, take all you want.

So they took everything they could find in the cell and started off. But they left behind a little bag that was hidden in the cell. The elder picked it up and followed after them, crying out: My son, take this, you forgot it in the cell! Amazed at the patience of the elder, they brought back everything into his cell and did penance, saying: This one really is a man of God.

The Way of the Desert

DAY TWELVE

Fasting

SCRIPTURE: Isaiah 58:3–8. Hypocritical and true fasting

Prayer

Heavenly Father:
Your most dear Son became incarnate and took upon himself
  fasting and grief, sorrow and sin-bearing;
Grant that we may follow him in his deprivation and in his
  joy, that we may share the blessedness of contentment in
  our present life and glory in the life to come;
For his dear name's sake. Amen.

Reflection

I've never thought of myself as an ascetic. The seeming
ascetic virtues that I practise are either accidental or
circumstantial. I am teetotal because I was brought up as
a Baptist (though there are even changes there now) and used
to stand solemnly with my hand raised at Band of Hope
meetings and earnestly declare with scores of other children:
"I promise, by divine assistance, to abstain from all
intoxicating liquors, and to encourage others to do the
same." I was ten years of age. And apart from trying the
Swiss-German beer when I lived in Zürich (it didn't take)
and lapses into brandy butter over my Christmas pud a few
years ago, I remain a teetotaller.

  Although Baptists are now more lax about alcohol,
smoking is still frowned upon and has become a great social

sin among secularists. As for my vegetarianism, that is a more personal thing, of a package with my pacifism and an increasing "green" perspective, having little to do with ascetic virtues. This leaves me little to give up during Lent!

I must say I'm impatient and critical of people who give up sugar and chocolate for the penitential period – it seems to me like an excuse for a dietary measure. If you are serious about Lent why not give up using your car (if you have one) for all but necessary journeys; why not give up tobacco or other drugs completely; why not give up going out for fancy meals and give the money to the hungry; or why not fast from food, sex or gossip on a regular basis?

Fasting is found in ancient Egyptian, Persian, Greek and Roman religion; in Shinto, Taoism, Confucianism, Hinduism, Islam, Judaism and Christianity. Jesus fasted and said that his disciples would do so.

In Judaism it was associated with definite occasions. Soldiers fasted in mourning and after defeat; people fasted in times of danger and to commemorate deliverances, before great undertakings and in intercession. There was fasting as a token of repentance or to avert judgement, and there were great national and liturgical times of fasting such as on the eve of Passover or the Day of Atonement.

Much of this thinking passed into Christian practice, though Jesus was scathing about hypocritical fasting and stood in the prophetic tradition of today's reading. Commenting on the current practice he said:

When you fast, do not look sombre as the hypocrites do, for they disfigure their faces to show men they are fasting. I tell you the truth, they have received their reward in full. But when you fast, put oil on your head and wash your face, so that it will not be obvious to men that you are fasting, but only to your Father, who is unseen; and your Father, who sees what is done in secret, will reward you. (Matthew 6:16–18)

The basic idea in fasting is abstinence or deprivation, and this may be not only from food and drink, but from sleep, drugs, luxurious living or sexual intercourse for specific periods of time in order to express repentance, sincere petition and to turn the attention away from mundane pleasure towards God in a concentrated manner.

The idea to participate in the solidarity of suffering with the oppressed may figure in fasting for deprived or afflicted societies. In the desert tradition the asceticism of the spiritual athlete was to the fore – the voluntary giving up of luxuries and even necessities for the sake of the spiritual race and crown:

> Everyone who competes in the games goes into strict training. They do it to get a crown that will not last; but we do it to get a crown that will last for ever. Therefore I do not run like a man running aimlessly; I do not fight like a man beating the air. No, I beat my body and make it my slave so that after I have preached to others, I myself will not be disqualified for the prize. (1 Corinthians 9:25–27)

I have said that I don't think of myself as an ascetic and that circumstances dictate much of my asceticism, though the more simply I live the more simply I *want* to live. My food supply is basic but adequate and does not include puddings and pastries, sweets, alcohol or tobacco. I do have access to fruit and eggs and use dried milk, and suppose that my one vice is instant coffee. I observe a Friday fast from solid food, but in all this there is not deprivation but delight, for there is such a thing as the joy of repentance.

The fact is that I do not eat meat or fish for a number of reasons, not least because I do not want to kill unnecessarily. I don't drink alcohol because of upbringing and I have no taste for it and could not afford it anyway. I don't smoke because I think it is unhealthy and revolting and I don't eat sweets because I don't like (most of) them, though I do like chocolate. Robert van de Weyer in a chapter on "Food" in *The Way of Holiness* writes of the primitive diet of the monastic life and its challenge to our processed, refined and unnatural eating habits:

> Our challenge is to re-educate our palates, so that we enjoy and relish the primitive diet. Aelred in the twelfth century wrote a moving description of the trauma he suffered moving from the king's palace in Scotland, where he held high office, to the monastery at Rievaulx: the hard bed, the rough clothes and the manual labour he could endure: but the dark bread, the thick lentil soup and the tough cabbage leaves made death by starvation seem attractive. Yet as Aelred and every other monk has found, after a few months the palate and the stomach adjust, so that natural foods actually give greater pleasure.

In these days there is a revival of the practice of fasting both from a spiritual and a secular perspective. In the secular world (and Christians are part of that world too) we are much more aware of the dangers of overindulgence, high blood-cholesterol, chemical fertilizers, food additives, processed and refined foods, not to speak of "mad cow" disease. The science of nutrition informs us and the science of toxicology warns us. We are all learning the value of giving the digestive system a sabbath rest, for a weekly fast is good even for atheists!

New Testament Christianity with its roots in Judaism commended personal and communal fasting. The Church incorporated into its discipline fasts in Lent and Advent, plus Wednesday and Friday fasting.

The Reformation churches could not deny its biblical character but allowed it to fall into some neglect, perhaps for fear of it gaining a meritorious aura contributing to salvation by works. But evangelical, sacramental and charismatic renewal over the last few decades have recognized its value in any contemporary spirituality.

For me, not only is it a token of repentance and participation with the fasting, sorrowing Jesus, but it unites me with the prophetic and apostolic tradition, with the ascetic athletes of the desert, and gives me a sense of solidarity with the suffering Church and world in these days of violence, hunger, persecution and deprivation.

We all need a faith which has backbone and an element of sacrifice in it. The gospel is meant to be a source of comfort and shelter in time of weakness and need, but it is no tranquillizer or opium to lull us into a false security while the major part of the world is experiencing hell.

We are all aware of the surfeit of superfluous goods in the "developed" world which encourages destruction of crops and harvests to keep prices and demand up while gross malnutrition leads most "undeveloped" countries to death. And we are continually exposed to the advertising media's manic efforts to create further "needs" for unnecessary products in such a mad world.

This theme of fasting is not meant to pile up guilt but rather to encourage us in the joy of sacrifice on our part, personally and communally, which pays dividends elsewhere. If you take this path your body will become healthier and you will appreciate basic and nourishing food all the more.

Response

* Keep a record of the *actual* main meals you eat during the next week, and their possible cost (including eating out).

* Make a record of the *possible* basic and healthy meals you could eat in a week and their cost. Compare and contrast.

* Make a simple resolution. Either initiate a fasting meal (or day) per week or clear out of your larder the superfluous or harmful foods and do not buy any more.

To Keep a True Lent

Is this a Fast, to keep
    The larder lean?
        And clean
From fat of veals and sheep?

Is it to quit the dish
    Of flesh, yet still
        To fill
The platter high with fish?

Is it to fast an hour,
    Or ragg'd to go,
        Or show
A down-cast look and sour?

No: 'tis a Fast to dole
    Thy sheaf of wheat
        And meat
Unto the hungry soul.

It is to fast from strife
    And old debate,

Fasting

And hate;
To circumcise thy life.

To show a heart grief-rent;
  To starve thy sin,
      Not bin;
And that's to keep thy Lent.

ROBERT HERRICK

DAY THIRTEEN

Relaxing

SCRIPTURE: Psalms 23, 37. Resting in the Lord

Prayer

*Yours is the abiding peace of eternity in which we shall
ultimately dwell, O Lord. Our present lives are often feverish
and irritable and our peace ill-founded and transient. Let
us not resort to techniques which pander to psychological
gimmicks and centre only on ourselves, but lead us to peace
through the forgiving love of our Lord Jesus and the healing
power of your Holy Spirit;*
Through the merits and grace of Christ our Lord. Amen.

Reflection

Are you happy with your temperament? I know many people
who are not, and they often project an aura of anger,
depression, obstinacy or fear. Some display a levity which
isn't real humour or joy, or they are bitchy, sarcastic, bossy
or cynical in order to cover up a basic insecurity.

I don't go in for birth signs or zodiac readings but my
libra picture is one of balanced scales. I don't know that
I'm temperamentally like that for I think of myself as extreme
in many of my perspectives, but there is one thing that has
done me the world of good – and that is learning a simple
technique of relaxation.

I didn't learn it in order to combat my sanguine excitability
or as an antidote to stress and anxiety, but as a preparation

and aid to contemplative prayer. The laid-back attitude which has been the result is a good side-effect of the main purpose, but I'm very grateful for it.

In the past many people have thought of me as a workaholic and a talkative zealot. It is certainly true that I have always admired spontaneity and been possessed of a lively imagination, glorying in being an optimistic enthusiast. In the first flush of my love for Jesus I often acted in zeal without knowledge but always managed to stop short of fanaticism. Being a Baptist I was in a "half-way house" between the charismatic (pentecostal) and the contemplative (catholic), enjoying the spontaneous liberty of the former while sneaking into the anglo-catholic church of St Gabriel's, Swansea, to savour its incense-laden atmosphere and to kneel in prayer before the reserved sacrament.

I am not knocking any of these traditions but indicating the mix that was part of my own temperament and the value of integrating a middle way which incorporated the best of the different emphases.

What people who didn't really know me did not understand was that when the public light went off and I left the pulpit, the lecture stand or the youth group, I was able to switch off immediately, slow my breathing and let my blood-pressure descend to a lower level. A little stress is good for you, both keeping you on your toes and enabling you to relax when the pressure is off. If I had not been able to do this I should have been pacing up and down worrying about the last or next engagement, muscles tense, anxiety-level high, with workaholic symptoms, making everyone else's life a misery.

So there was this ability to switch on/switch off for which I was grateful to the Lord. But nature and grace needed to run together, and I realized that there was sometimes the tendency to carry too much, not to be able to say "no" and too much of a desire to be liked – which always leads to projecting a positive image — and that is as exhausting as indulging in duplicity.

The fact that my prayer life was not right was both a symptom and a disease. I had been reading in the mystical and contemplative tradition for years and I knew that any real prescription must come from that dimension. It was not simply a technique that I needed but radical surgery, though a simple technique or method was the way in.

I had met enough charismatic enthusiasts to know that for my temperament an over-exposure to that tradition could lead to superficiality and the evasion of the dark night. But I had also met enough pious and neurotic catholics (anglo and roman) to know the temptation and lure of wearing the dark night upon one's sleeve. Off-beat humour needed to be mixed with serious intention, as Rabbi Lionel Blue indicates in some sound advice on "Blues in the Night":

> Sitting back in your chair you can try some contemplation. Play with it. Don't take it too heavy — St Teresa didn't always, so why should you? Just watch some clouds of unknowing drifting by. Work out if you're in the third or fourth mansion of the Interior Castle or just stuck in the castle moat — and that's more interesting than sheep, isn't it? Your night of the soul may be dark, but it doesn't have to be dreary.

This enables us not to take ourselves too seriously — only God is to be taken ultimately seriously, and he is the source of humour and joy.

I do not want to lay out a contemplative technique here, but I do emphasize the importance of learning a technique of relaxation. We do not relax properly. Our posture is strained, our breathing is shallow and our body language full of tension. There are many underlying causes for this, and a relaxation technique does not deal with many of these, but it can enable us to find a new direction and come to a truer diagnosis of our condition.

Religious people are not the most relaxed. Both in charismatic conventions and catholic retreats it is possible to meet frenetic activists full of anxieties and recompensing spiritual practices which only exacerbate the situation. For instance the fear of silence or the desire to dance or continually sing choruses indicates a lack of interior stillness before God. And a pious fussiness and clamour for introspective spiritual direction in some retreat-goers indicate a lack of resting in the unqualified loving acceptance of God.

Both these kinds of people live too much in their heads, neglecting an appreciation of the bodily sensations that keep us in the present moment. They are often worrying or gloating over the past or dreaming, dreading and anticipating the future. There's nothing wrong in learning from past mistakes nor in positively planning and working towards a positive future, as long as the present moment is not neglected.

One of the basic and best books on methods of prayer that involve body, mind and spirit is Anthony de Mello's *Sadhana: A Way to God*, which is a book of Christian exercises in a meditative mode. Its value lies in the fact that here is a trustworthy Christian teacher who can communicate the *practical* nature of prayer, showing simply *how to do it*.

The first section of the book is an invitation to practise bodily awareness involving sensation, posture, breathing, stillness and concentration, all laid out with practical exercises. These are the kind of exercises I learned for myself by experimentation and was delighted when I found that "my way" was in fact part of a universal intuitive method prescribed for a discovery of the body and mind in relation to prayer.

Our relaxation theme today concludes with one of his awareness exercises and this can lead into a meditation upon one of today's psalms. Both these psalms speak of resting in God, letting go physical and mental tension in the simple trust between sheep and shepherd. You can think of yourself as a sheep wandering in the luscious green pastures of God's provision or by the still waters of his peace and love, with the security and protection afforded by the watchful and caring shepherd.

Or you can think of yourself as David wandering over the hillside with his flock under the guidance of the heavenly Shepherd – now moving into greener pastures, now resting in the evening stillness, now playing upon his shepherd's pipe, now calling and leading the sheep back to the security of the fold for the dark hours of the night.

All this indicates an attitude of relaxed trust, of abandonment to the will and pleasure of God, of a sense of inward peace and tranquillity which is communicated to the flock and which is grounded in the divine love.

It is clear that no contemporary Christian can be unaware or unconcerned about social issues. We are all involved with our fellow human beings, and though we may not choose a party political involvement, a proportion of our time, energy and money must be channelled into compassionate action. But there are dangers if such moral responsibility becomes our primary task with little transcendent dimension. Our gospel has definite social implications but it is not simply a social gospel.

The contemporary Christian must be theological, social *and* contemplative. The integration of a disciplined time of silence and meditation is more necessary now than ever to undergird the social and theological superstructure. Without contemplation a Christian man or woman can become either a frenetic social activist ending up with a paralysis caused by compassion fatigue or stress, or can become coldly dogmatic and cerebral, leading to bigotry and exclusivism. A relaxed tranquillity is the base from which theological affirmation and social concern should operate. Otherwise when the rain descends and the floods beat upon the house, the super-structure will collapse, lacking a contemplative foundation.

I speak like this from a hermitage in which solitude is primary – a seeming anomaly when the Church is aware as never before of the world as the global village, and the ecological, military and economic concerns of the world are part of the Church's prayer and work.

Yet this makes my plea for tranquillity and interior peace all the more urgent, for unless this is a primary personal concern it cannot become a corporate one. And if it is not a corporate concern then the Church will become another warring political or social faction, impotent before the immensity and intractability of the problems.

I am here surrounded by the peace and tranquillity of solitude and therefore able to enter in empathy and prayer into the multifarious concerns of Church and the world. And you, my reader, are in that busy and engaging area of Church and marketplace which needs your active love and attention. Therefore we must pool our resources as various ministries within the one Body of Christ, so that it will truly be *from* each according to her ability, and *to* each according to his need.

Response

* Write down areas of your life in which you feel weariness, stress and even exhaustion, and then those areas in which you feel freedom, space, and a sense of relaxation and tranquillity.

* Show the writing to a spouse/friend and ask them to comment.

* If you practise no daily meditative discipline, set about seeking a person or group with whom you can learn a basic meditative technique.

Body Sensations

Take up a posture that is comfortable and restful. Close your eyes. Now I am going to ask you to become aware of certain sensations in your body that you are feeling at this moment, but of which you are not explicitly aware . . . Be aware of the touch of your clothes on your shoulders . . . Now become aware of the touch of your clothes on your back, or of your back touching the chair you are sitting on . . . Now be aware of the feel of your hands as they touch each other or rest on your lap . . . Now become conscious of your thighs or your buttocks pressing against your chair . . . Now the feel of your feet touching your shoes . . . Now become explicitly aware of your sitting posture . . .

Once again: your shoulders . . . your back . . . your right hand . . . your left hand . . . your thighs . . . your feet . . . your sitting posture . . .

Again: shoulders . . . back . . . right hand . . . left hand . . . right thigh . . . left thigh . . . right foot . . . left foot . . . sitting posture . . .

Continue to go the round by yourself now, moving from one part of your body to the other. Do not dwell for more than a couple of seconds on each part, shoulders, back, thighs, etc. . . . . Keep moving from one to the other. You may dwell either on the parts of the body I have indicated or on any other parts you wish: your head, your neck, your arms, your chest, your stomach . . . The important thing is that you get the *feel*, the sensation of each part, that you feel it for a second or two and then move on to another part of the body . . .

After five minutes I shall ask you to open your eyes gently and end the exercise.

ANTHONY DE MELLO

Part II

MIND

DAY FOURTEEN

Obeying

SCRIPTURE: Hebrews 11:8–19. Abraham's faith and obedience

Prayer

When I call you Master or Lord, I do not think of you as tyrant or despot but as my loving Father who gently receives the obedience of his child. You call me back from my wayward wandering and set my feet aright; You call me forward into new ways of service and responsibility; You call me inward into unimagined depths of loving communion. Grant to me an unfolding awareness of your purpose and a loving obedience to your will. For in your will is my peace. Amen.

Reflection

There is a threefold monastic vow: poverty, chastity (or celibacy) and obedience. Poverty is not negative penury but the desire to own nothing, sharing a simple life, and is a gospel witness in a materialistic society. Celibacy is not coldness but the desire to consecrate the profound depths of love and sexuality to God and to people while surrendering a specific genital relationship. This is a relationship witness in a sex-obsessed society. Obedience is the surrender to God's will directly, through the Spirit's voice in Scripture and community. This is a disciplined witness in a self-orientated society.

That all sounds very grand but it is not so simple. The first two are difficult enough, though there is immense joy in their positive fulfilment. But obedience is even more difficult and sometimes complicated, for "the will of God" is not always clear! Part of me rebels against the very notion of a vowed obedience, especially in a monastic context. My Celtic spirit of rebellion and independence will give obedience to no man or woman, for personal freedom is the basis of corporate liberty.

Even when community obedience is more clearly the will of God the notion is still foreign to my understanding of the gospel which is a free response to a universal call of love. And then when my *thinking* compels me to obedience my *feelings* rebel!

But perhaps it is necessary to distinguish between different kinds of obedience, for there is all the difference in the world between law and grace.

The kind which makes my hackles rise is *slavish obedience* – that demanded by a tyrant or overlord, with penalties for refusal – whether in secular or religious garb. It is a moral duty to resist such totalitarian regimes, and that is why secular and religious martyrs have gone singing to seal such witness with their blood. "We must obey God rather than men," countered Peter and the other apostles when the religious authorities forbade them to witness to Christ and demanded obedience.

Any obedience which is rendered out of fear or based in punishment ought not to be submitted to. Any state or religious authority demanding such obedience is not worthy of it, and should be resisted.

But what about military obedience? Recently a book entitled *Wellington the Iron Duke* was reviewed in which it was said that "he stamped his will upon his army". There are those – the majority I suppose – who affirm that there can be no conditional obedience to a military command in time of war, otherwise the force would be in disarray, giving the battle to the enemy. Military training and practice must be based on obedience unquestioned, and this leads to the idea of "my country, right or wrong" which was voiced by a military general and a cardinal during the Vietnam war! How different was Dietrich Bonhoeffer's understanding of obedience during the Nazi regime which led him to the concentration camp and death — for treason!

Military obedience is too large a problem to tackle here, so it will have to go into parenthesis — but it is clear the direction I would take if there was a conflict between the demands of God and earthly authorities.

Then there is *legal obedience* which ought to be given, though it falls far short of a joyful and glad assent, and smells too much of duty. The law-making process compels us to common assent, sometimes against our inclinations, for the common and greater good. In any civilized society there often has to be some personal surrender for the good of others, though it may be irksome. This applies to the obeying of traffic lights, refraining from alcohol when driving and covers all the social and domestic duties that make life easier for us and our fellows. This is a social and moral necessity, of course, and there are times when we have to grin and bear it, in doing something or refraining from something for the sake of others.

Sometimes the apostle of free grace sounds somewhat legalistic in his demands: "Wives, submit to your husbands . . . children obey your parents . . . slaves obey your masters . . . husbands love your wives" (Ephesians 5:22, 25; 6:1, 5). He admits that he wrote his first letter to the Corinthians to test them: "The reason I wrote to you was to see if you would stand the test and be obedient in everything" (2 Corinthians 2:9).

But St Paul can be greatly misunderstood and he *must* be read in context, for every call to obedience is surrounded by tears, rejoicing and a freedom that is unsurpassed in its vision of grace. He was also the exponent of such gospel liberty that made religious legalists accuse him of licence. The middle way is precarious.

Then there is what I would call *wisdom obedience*, which is the counsel of the master or teacher who knows the discipline and whose call to obedience is for the instruction of the initiate in his/her training to perfection.

This applies to the moral life, to an art or craft, to athletic training or to spiritual pilgrimage. There is an agreed and traditional "way" and obedience is the joyful submission to the discipline which leads to maturity or perfection in the task or journey.

Sometimes there is warning-counsel if you do not obey, but this is not punishment but chastisement and correction, just as a loving parent will discipline a child in love, though it is not appreciated at the time! (Hebrews 12:5–13).

This brings us to *loving obedience*. This is the essence of the gospel, for it is a call to harmonize with the will of God which is joyfully perceived and assented to by the hearer. All the commands of Jesus are calls to loving obedience and issue in forgiveness, rest, peace, hope, illumination, meaning and joyful service – in a word, salvation. This is set out clearly in the great invitation of Matthew 11:28–30:

> Come to me, all you who are weary and burdened, and I will give you rest. Take my yoke upon you and learn from me, for I am gentle and humble in heart, and you will find rest for your souls. For my yoke is easy and my burden is light.

There are those who think of religious obedience as paralleled by military obedience. Both the Jesuit Order and the Salvation Army come to mind. I remember chuckling at the words of the Jesuit Superior in the film *The Mission*, when he said: "This is an Order, not a Democracy!"

But this way of thinking seems to me to place the yoke of legalistic bondage upon the monastic witness and gave some reason for the contempt of many monks and friars in the corrupt Church of medieval times and the suppression of the monasteries during the Reformation. Here is God's call to obedience mingled with a drastic warning:

> I know your deeds, that you are neither cold nor hot. I wish you were either one or the other! So because you are lukewarm – neither hot nor cold – I am about to spit you out of my mouth . . . Those whom I love I rebuke and discipline. So be in earnest, and repent (Revelation 3:15–16, 19).

In the book *Brother Edward: Priest and Evangelist* there is a letter which Edward, who had tested his vocation in an Anglican Religious Order, wrote to his sister. He spoke of a negative kind of obedience which he had found and of his suspicions of *this* vow as bolstering up the political and ecclesial power of the monastic life:

> I cannot help thinking that in its essence it is Judaistic, the sort of danger that St Paul contended against in Galatians . . . There were people living under special vows in the Church before the associating of them together into communities, when for the frailty of nature a third vow of obedience was had recourse to. My contention . . . is that this may be needed as a mortification of self-will, but is not a counsel of perfection on all-fours with the call to celibacy and poverty, which we have our Lord's own word for. It is when it is exalted to this level that I run up against it.

When the monastic tradition is true to Scripture it is in touch with the loving obedience exercised by Abraham when he heard the call of God to leave Ur of the Chaldees and to travel into the unknown (Genesis 12:1-9). This act of obedience is taken up in the Letter to the Hebrews illustrating the life of faith (11:8-19). And the same letter gives us a humbling glimpse of the humanity of Jesus in his obedience:

> During the days of Jesus' life on earth, he offered up prayers and petitions with loud cries and tears to the one who could save him from death, and he was heard because of his reverent submission. Although he was a son, he learned obedience from what he suffered and, once made perfect, he became the source of eternal salvation for all who obey him (5:7-9).

I've mentioned my own difficulties with obedience. When I was about nineteen I had an AJS 350cc motor cycle, but coveted a Triumph 500cc twin cylinder, reduced in price in a local motor cycle shop at the end of the season. As I gazed at it I heard quite plainly, without equivocation, the single word "No!" A divine negative!

In spite of this I determined to have it. So I gave my AJS in part-exchange with hire-purchase agreement and took delivery of the Triumph. It was all I hoped it would be, surpassing my expectations, so there was no mechanical or aesthetic reason for me to be unhappy or uncomfortable. But I was. For one thing, I always sent up an arrow-prayer when getting on to my motor bike, but I could no longer do that. I sped along the road eating up the miles with a tremendous feeling of exhilaration, but with a heavy shadow upon my heart.

Eventually – was it a month? – I had to take it back, losing money I could not afford. I ended up with a small BSA 125cc two-stroke Bantam. Enough to depress any motor cyclist! But the burden lifted and I was happy again. It was the cost of obedience, but after that I learned to mingle *wisdom obedience* with *loving obedience*. And that's where I am as I write these words. How about you?

Response

* How far is obedience part of the discipline of your Christian life?

* Have you learned from past disobedience, and do you experience joy in obeying the will of God?

* Write down three headings: 1) *Personal Obedience* (your own will); 2) *Corporate Obedience* (family, community, church); 3) *Obedience to God*. Under each heading evaluate how you *feel* and how you *act* in respect of each.

The word *obedience* comes from the Latin root *audire* – to hear, to listen. The prefix, making it *ob-audire* signifies *intent and alert listening*, so that the powers of heart and concentration are given to the action. This is the way in which Jesus listened, and he learned obedience from what he suffered. True obedience is not a slavish assent to an external command, it is rather a loving, and sometimes a suffering, response to the love of God – and only love can answer love.

DAY FIFTEEN

Struggling

SCRIPTURE: Romans 8:18–27. The travail of creation

Prayer

Creator and Redeemer God:
You made us in your own image and redeemed us through
  Jesus your Son:
Look with compassion on the whole human family;
cleanse away the hatred and arrogance that infect us;
break down the walls of enmity that separate us;
in our difficulties and struggles waylay us;
uphold and sustain us that we may at last attain to your
  kingdom of love and peace;
Through Jesus Christ our Lord. Amen.

Reflection

I really don't know what I'd make of the world as it appears in all its glory and pain if I had not entered into the experience of forgiveness, redemption and the compassion of Christ.

There are certainly times even now when I find myself struggling to understand, sometimes feeling, like the psalmist, that I am sinking up to my neck in the mire. Kierkegaard the philosopher said that life can only be understood backwards, but it must be lived forwards. Looking back on many experiences I can see now a very clear and beautiful pattern where previously there were

sighings and tears. It is the perspective of faith and love –
where I believe that God gives me an experience of the
groaning of creation which is described in the eighth chapter
of the Letter to the Romans.

In one of my solitude reports to my spiritual director I
wrote about part of this struggle, reflecting on evil in the
world, the predatory nature of some animals and the
seemingly impassive aspect of nature:

1 Evil in the world. The whole Gulf crisis erupted since
   my coming here, and that, together with the present
   threatened Kurdish massacres which are the aftermath,
   have catapulted me into new confrontation with the
   nature of humankind and evil. I know this has been
   the case for all Christians and people of goodwill and
   has shaken us all up, but here, alone – and especially
   in the hour or two of darkness from 4.30 a.m. I have
   been engulfed by it, shaken by it, in tears because of it.

2 The predatory nature of creatures. One morning some
   months ago I went up at about 6.30 a.m. to do my
   daily job of feeding/watering/cleaning the hens which
   are usually clucking with great anticipation when they
   hear my clanking pails. There was deathly silence and
   no movement. I found the flap open in one henhouse
   and some of the hens huddled together in the corner,
   terrified, and around the hen-run little piles of feathers
   – all that remained of seven chickens, including the
   proud and noisy bantam cock. The fox had been and
   found the open flap. These surviving hens would not
   come out, would not feed, and it took days to get them
   back to some routine again. I know such things are
   taken in the stride of an ordinary farmer/poultry-
   keeper, but such things are significant for me in the
   context of prayer and solitude.

3 The impassive aspect of nature. Apart from "nature red in tooth and claw" as described above, there is the impassive and seeming cruelty of some aspects. One morning in the ten degrees below zero temperatures we had this winter I found a large ewe who had fallen into a hollow and through the night had frozen to death. Again, just another incident which a countryman may make no fuss about – but for me it indicated that "other side" of nature which I have often waxed so lyrical about – a nature pervaded by beauty, harmony, balance, design – a kind of existential teleological argument! Of course there is nothing new for me here, but to face it like this is to face it anew. Then to carry it down into prayer and meditation is to work through it again. It is to question the whole fabric of my theology and philosophy of life again, in the quest for true and real attitudes.

What happens to me sometimes in prayer is that I am confronted by one or more aspects of the ambiguity of our world, of nature, of creatures, of humankind, so that there is a kind of struggle, wrestling, entering into conflict with such darkness, so that in the love and power of Christ it may be redeemed. It is the redeeming love of Christ working itself out in my prayer, and that can only be prayer as a gift – the Holy Spirit praying in and through me. "The Spirit helps us in our weakness. We do not know what we ought to pray for, but the Spirit himself intercedes for us with groans that words cannot express" (Romans 8:26).

If *that* happens, then from the conflict emerges not a sense of weakness but of victory, as if the dark powers are put to flight and the *meaning* of redemption is lived out in my experience in solitude here in the darkness, in the loneliness, in and through the pain. Human weakness is charged with divine power. That, I think, is the beginning of union with God – what the Orthodox saints call *theosis* – the life of God filling, redeeming, sanctifying my soul.

And that is part of this solitude. I can only live at this level if I am alone. I do not speak for others who may carry all this together with the social and ministering aspects of their lives. But just now, in order to enter ever more deeply into such struggle, I need to be alone to be able to weep aloud, or laugh or dance or sing in ways which would be thought of as mad – or at least as eccentric!

Response

* Are you *honest* in your thinking about sin and evil in the world? Do you put a theological lid upon it all or make doctrinal excuses in order to justify God (*your* theology!) when you really feel the ambiguity of it all deep in your heart?

* Are you able to be *honest* in God's presence in prayer? Can you simply lay yourself before God in all your pain and weakness, your unbelief and inability to comprehend the sin and sorrow of our poor world?

* Calvary portrays God suffering at the heart of creation. Is this a way of seeing that suffering is not the final word? Use this as a starting point and reflect upon the following words:

Suffering with God

Struggling and suffering was part of the pilgrimage of Jesus, for his path to glory carried him through the *Via Dolorosa* – the Way of Sorrows. The call to discipleship is no easy option, for the disciple can only tread in the steps of the Master, and the only real discipleship involves the believer in struggle and pain. But this is not negative or destructive suffering – it is creative, redemptive and even joyful.

There is no suffering we can encounter that Jesus has not experienced before us, and no depths that he has not plumbed. Wherever human beings are lonely, imprisoned, tortured, hungry, thirsty, dispossessed or dying – there Jesus suffers too – and there Jesus redeems human suffering.

In Jesus, suffering touches the heart of God, and Jesus' tears are the weeping of the Almighty. God became part of our suffering in order that we may become sharers of his glory. If our suffering participates in the groaning and birth-pangs of travail described in the eighth chapter of Romans, then we shall be caught up into the glory and splendour of a new creation in which all suffering will be redeemed and transfigured. For "I consider that our present sufferings are not worth comparing with the glory that will be revealed in us" (Romans 8:18).

Missing

SCRIPTURE: Matthew 26:36–56. The loneliness of Jesus

Prayer

God my Father, Lover and Friend:
When I rejoice in human love, let me see your face in the
*   loved one;*
When I grieve in the loneliness of love lost, be near me in
*   the darkness;*
When human friends fail, and my heart is cold and lonely,
*   then let me learn your solitude,*
*   and in that solitude find your peace;*
Through Jesus Christ my Lord. Amen.

Reflection

"Then all the disciples deserted him and fled." There are
two incidents in the life of Jesus which make me tremble
every time I hear or read them. They contain the height and
depth of his singularity, and radiate a numinous quality of
awe and bewilderment. They are the stories of Jesus'
transfiguration on the mountain, and his pain and heaviness
in the Garden of Gethsemane. In the former story we read
of *Jesus only* and in the latter of *Jesus alone.*

In both these stories the disciples Peter, James and John
are *near* but not *with* Jesus, for they fall asleep. – at Tabor
because they were unable to face the outshining glory and
in Gethsemane because they were full of fear. At Tabor it

was *Jesus only* in the radiance of his solitude. The words in the text are *Iesous monos*, and *monos* is the word used later for the solitude of the monk of the desert. The blazing glory and effulgence of the Holy Spirit radiated from Jesus' body, for the Spirit was given to him without measure.

But the solitude of Gethsemane was loneliness, for it was there that he entered into the beginnings of his dereliction which was brought to its consummation in those fearful words from the Cross: "My God, my God, why have you forsaken me?" (Matthew 27:46). Already in Gethsemane the disciples had forsaken him in spirit because they could not bear to face the harrowing loneliness of the deepening darkness which was engulfing them. And soon they would forsake him physically, for the crowd of soldiers and religionists led by Judas were already making their way to the olive grove. If Jesus ever needed human companionship and warmth he needed it then, but "all the disciples deserted him and fled."

There is no comparison between my darkness and his, but we all have to share the same pilgrimage to Calvary that he undertook. The path the Master walked must be followed by the servant, for though it is a path of suffering it is also a path of love. And a share in the solitude and loneliness of Jesus is part of the pattern for every disciple.

For years I longed for solitude, for I was lonely in the midst of people. I remember clearly seeking the solitude of sea and country from my school friends as a child. As the years have progessed I have continued to value solitude, for then I was most myself and closer to that sense of *presence* which has ever surrounded and engulfed my being.

Yet now having found such solitude the paradox is that I feel myself afraid, as the disciples did. I am afraid because I am unable to be exposed to the transfiguring holiness of God in the nakedness of my mortal being. And I am afraid because I cannot face the bleak darkness of lonely suffering

that lies upon the road to ultimate union with the divine
Love. There is no union without purgation and the way to
glory takes the *Via Dolorosa* of Calvary.

> Eternal Light! eternal Light!
>   How pure the soul must be
> When, placed within Thy searching sight,
>   It shrinks not, but with calm delight
> Can live and look on Thee . . .
>
> O how shall I, whose native sphere
>   Is dark, whose mind is dim,
> Before the ineffable appear,
>   And on my naked spirit bear
> The uncreated beam?

There is paradox here because I *wanted* the solitude. Indeed
it became *imperative* that I sought it because without it I
could make no more progress upon the particular path to
which I felt drawn. But it was not a path which should cut
me off from fellow human beings, but rather a way of
learning to love them more and at a deeper level.

Solitude may include loneliness as it did in the experience
of Jesus, but it does not mean isolation. Isolation is negative
and may be the result of cynicism or even hatred of others;
and if solitude should degenerate into isolation the soul is
in great danger. John Cassian warns of a premature and ill-
prepared flight into solitude: "If we retire to solitude or secret
places, without our faults being first cured, their operation
is but repressed, while the power of feeling them is not
extinguished." And as Thomas Merton points out: "True
solitude is the home of the person, false solitude is the refuge
of the individualist."

Therefore, my solitude, though it calls for a necessary
detachment and interior freedom to see things in true
perspective, and though it enables me to see myself more

clearly in my emptiness and potential, and though it provides the place where the Lord makes himself more present to my inmost soul, yet it leads me into a certain loneliness.

I mean this first of all in a simple and basic missing of friends and loved ones. How often over the last two years I have longed to share joy and sorrow, laughter and tears – but I am alone. One of the basic creative joys of being human is to be able to turn to a loved one and weep with him or laugh with her. The human linking of hands, warm embrace, side by side or face to face, is so precious that we only realize the depth of such actions when we lose them.

It is difficult to speak for others and I would not presume to understand the path of another sister or brother walking a solitary path, but for me it is true that I greatly miss people, want people, need people. Anything that Barbra Streisand sings is all right with me, but especially:

> People who need people
> are the luckiest people in the world . . .
> Lovers are very special people,
> They're the luckiest people in the world.
> With one person, one very special person,
> A feeling deep in your soul
> Says you were half, now you're whole,
> No more hunger and thirst,
> But first be a person who needs people . . .

and this is complemented in the sadness of Ella Fitzgerald singing: "Every time we say goodbye/I die a little . . ."

The New Testament is quite clear when it says that no one can love God who has not first loved his brother or sister. If my solitude leads to isolation then I am on the path of darkness. But if my solitude leads to compassion and fellowship then I am on the path of light where love draws everyone to itself.

My first two years of the present solitude have been strict

100

in that, with two or three exceptions, I have seen only my spiritual director and a few members of my community. During the second year I had an increasing number of letters from people who *wanted* to see me, and some who *needed* to come to talk, to pray, to share the pain and joy of their particular pilgrimage. My immediate disciplined response was to say "no" in as gentle a way as possible and to explain the nature of this present solitude.

On two occasions it seemed clear that I should see the people, and not only did it turn out to be right but they felt a sense of pervading peace in this enclosure and I felt the warmth and embrace of their friendship and love as we shared anxieties and depressions, hopes and expectations. Experiences such as these make me believe that the person who truly understands gospel celibacy is the one who would love to be a mother or father, and the person who enters into the deep places of solitude is the one who is capable of profound human love.

People who read what I write are sometimes single, sometimes deeply in love, sometimes married with families, sometimes having lost a loved one through relationship breakdown or bereavement, and sometimes a person who has mostly lived alone. I would be glad if all these people would enter more deeply into the solitude and communion which Jesus offers in the Gospels and which he now desires to share with the lonely and with lovers.

My paradox is that I long continually for ever-deepening solitude, but I also long for people – and for you who read these words now – because I am lonely in a simple, basic and human sense. Does this mean that the Lord is showing me that I should return to the marketplace, to overt ministry and fellowship? Perhaps.

But it is just as likely that the more I love and long for people, the more the Lord will lead me deeper into solitude for the same people. However that may be, missing people is part of my vocation, for as Jesus was never alone in his loneliness (John 16:32), so I shall endeavour to follow the pattern of his steps, even though I am afraid.

Response

* Do you value both loneliness and friendship as part of your human experience leading you to know God more intimately?

* Do you seek to evade the risk of human loving because of being hurt in the past? Do you realize the danger of becoming cold and cynical if you do not remain open to love?

* Reproduce in your journal the following passage by C.S. Lewis from his book *The Four Loves*, and let its implications remain with you through the day.

To love at all is to be vulnerable. Love anything and your heart will certainly be wrung and possibly be broken. If you want to be sure of keeping it intact, you must give your heart to no-one, not even to an animal. Wrap it carefully around with hobbies and little luxuries; avoid all entanglements; lock it up safe in the casket or coffin of your selfishness. But in that casket – safe, dark, motionless, airless – it will change. It will not be broken, it will become unbreakable, impenetrable, irredeemable. The alternative to tragedy is damnation. The only place outside heaven you can be safe from all the dangers and perturbations of love is hell.

C.S. LEWIS

DAY SEVENTEEN

Studying

SCRIPTURE: Proverbs 8:1–11; Wisdom of Solomon 7:15–30. The wisdom and knowledge of God

Prayer

All-loving God of Wisdom and Truth;
Your Holy Spirit lives and breathes through all things,
In him we live and move and have our being;
Enable us by his illumination and guidance to order our lives
*   wisely and compassionately, so that powers of mind and*
*   heart may be dedicated to your perfect will;*
Through Jesus Christ our Lord. Amen.

Reflection

St Francis was suspicious of learning, though it must be said that it was pride in book learning that he was afraid of. The scholarly reputation of the *litterati* friars often turned them from the simplicity of the love of God. The sad story of scholarly in-fighting, strife and eventual schism only proved Francis right, though there is the parallel story of friars whose minds, as well as their hearts, were dedicated to the love and wisdom of God.

It is a great pity that Christians, evangelical and catholic, are often not acquainted with the inter-testamental wisdom literature. The following passage is lifted from a beautiful section of the Wisdom of Solomon:

Wisdom is the radiance that streams from everlasting light, the flawless mirror of the active power of God, and the image of his goodness. She is but one, yet can do all things; herself unchanging, she makes all things new; age after age she enters into holy souls, and makes them friends of God and prophets, for nothing is acceptable to God but the person who makes his home with wisdom. She is more beautiful than the sun, and surpasses every constellation. Compared with the light of day, she is found to excel, for day gives place to night, but against wisdom no evil can prevail. She spans the world in power from end to end, and gently orders all things. (7:26–8:1 (REB)

A right understanding of true learning and study stimulates the Christian to see the wisdom and Spirit of God in all things true, good and beautiful. There is no area of art or science where the Spirit of God is not to be found, for where truth is, there is God. A wise monk once told me that a good monastery library should contain an *Introduction* to all the great world disciplines – from astronomy to woodwork, from physics to market gardening! The whole of creation is shot through with the wisdom and dynamic of God. I feel a profound intuitive response to all this and have not let go my reading and learning in all my experimentation with solitude, though I do realize that there may come a time when I shall be required to do without books.

My study disciplines over the past few years, apart from the text of biblical study, have kept me in touch with historical and contemporary theologians, mystical and spirituality traditions, and the contemplative and social applications of theology in the world.

It has always been a great joy to me to introduce young people to the excitement of theological study – in the parish, university chaplaincy and among novices in the community.

I have also tried to find place for reading in new disciplines which seem to have little to do with religion, and I enjoy controversial literature and debate – especially friendly encounter with the "opposition"! God is to be found everywhere, and in the most unlikely places. Nature and grace conspire together to manifest a scintillating display of glory in creation and redemption, in things physical, mental and spiritual.

Apart from any academic reading which has engaged me in this period of solitude, there is an increasing genre of writing which has delighted me, and which can be illustrated by Tolkien's *Lord of the Rings* or Richard Adams' *Watership Down*. I'd like to draw attention to a triology which has stimulated me to profound reflection, wholesome laughter, deep sorrow and sympathetic tears.

What a claim for one saga! I refer to the *Duncton Chronicles* by William Horwood – the story of some generations of moledom in which the deepest spiritual themes and disciplines of moledom (humanity) are pursued with an empathy and sagacity that reflects the ancient wisdoms underlying the greatest faiths and philosophies.

The first volume, *Duncton Wood*, sets the scene of a community of moles in the beauty of Duncton's changing seasons in the south of England. Within the cyclic and domestic pattern of a simple mole system we are made aware of the breathtaking beauty of colour and life, and the beginning of the process of evil, darkness and brute violence. So begins the pilgrimage and quest for healing and redemption in the lives of two ordinary but extraordinary moles, Bracken and Rebecca, and the emergence of the great White Mole Boswell who haunts the whole saga.

The second volume, *Duncton Quest*, lays the burden of the story upon Tryfan, the successor of Bracken, who companies Boswell to holy Uffington where the wise scribemoles are the custodians of the faith of the Stone. The Stone represents the transcendent mystery of Love, and it would be wrong to say more than that, save that I couldn't help but apply the whole chain of biblical references summed up in 1 Peter 2:6, "See, I lay a stone in Zion, a chosen and precious cornerstone, and the one who trusts in him will never be put to shame."

In the second volume the forces of darkness are encapsulated in a religion of the "Word" and personified in its evil master and mistress. The Word here is not the *logos* of wisdom and truth, but the *ratio* of power which leads to a totalitarian compulsion and control of all the mole systems and a crude use of violence to subjugate body and spirit completely.

Tryfan's wisdom is that of compassion and growth in longing for gentleness and non-violence in moledom. In the midst of grief and pain he continually lives and preaches compassion under persecution, proclaiming the coming of the Stone-mole who is the redeeming messiah figure who will lead the way into the mystical silence and love of the way of the Stone.

The third volume, *Duncton Found*, relates the progress of the powers of darkness under the evil mistress Henbane and master Lucerne, the persecution and massacre of the Stone followers and the birth, teaching, dying and undying of Beechen, the gentle but powerful Stone-mole who is truly a mole of sorrow and joy.

I know it seems strange, under the theme of "Studying" to commend a fantastic trilogy of this genre, but these Chronicles have ministered to every part of my being. They portray the physical and material elements of a social and political system, the intellectual stimulus of wisdom and philosophical thinking, and the spiritual profundity which reverberates with the mystical and spiritual truths of Christian faith at its best.

When I say that some of the deepest insights I have gained from my quest for God in prayer and solitude over the past two years have been reflected in this saga (well over 2,000 pages), then that is sufficient reason for its inclusion here.

I shall refer to the story elsewhere in these pages, but from the first volume comes a quotation which applies so clearly to many people who have come to me for counsel and help in their spiritual pilgrimage over the last two decades. Some of them have been bursting with enthusiasm and impatience, some bowed with discouragement and some smitten with grief, pain or disillusion. But all of them have come seeking help, illumination, strength and wisdom.

Rose the Healer is explaining to Rebecca the disciple how some questions are not capable of explanation until a certain moment, the right time, the mature season, when baffling problems give way to the understanding of wisdom, gentleness and love:

> A mole will come to know things if he's going to, and no amount of talking about it will make him understand if he's not going to. And even if he or she is going to get to know something, it's no good trying to hurry the process up – it happens when it's meant to and there's nothing you or I can do about it. Well, perhaps we can encourage it sometimes.

Response

* Have you learned to discern the difference between knowledge and wisdom so that knowledge may serve wisdom's deeper fulfilment?

* Do you believe that all truth is God's truth and that your intellectual powers should be dedicated to him?

* List areas of study in which you have worked during the past year, and the possible work and reading you hope to attempt during the next year.

God it was who gave me true understanding of things as they are: a knowledge of the structure of the world and the operation of the elements; the beginning and end of epochs and their middle course; the alternating solstices and changing seasons; the cycles of the years and the constellations; the nature of living creatures and behaviour of wild beasts; the violent force of winds and human thought; the varieties of plants and the virtues of roots. I learnt it all, hidden or manifest, for I was taught by wisdom, by her whose skill made all things. (Wisdom of Solomon 7:17–22 REB)

DAY EIGHTEEN

Guiding

SCRIPTURE: Acts 16:6–10. Waiting on the Lord

Prayer

Holy Spirit of God:
You have guided men and women through the ages,
leading them through hard and difficult places
to a new and promised land.
Grant us stillness of heart and mind,
a spirit of quiet receptivity,
that hearing your voice and made aware of your leading
we may follow humbly, obey willingly, and find at last
your perfect will;
Through Jesus Christ our Lord. Amen.

Reflection

Before I started on this present solitary path I was sometimes
besieged by people who were seeking help, counsel and
guidance for their lives. It was a joy to be involved with such
a ministry, but often I had to tell them just to *wait* upon
the Lord.

Their questions were often imperative. They wanted to
know why and where and how and when – and they
wanted to know now! I told them that if the Lord did not
intend to tell them it was no use them worrying, harrying,
pestering him – for that would only lead to frustration.

There have been times in my own pilgrimage when I have

been confronted with a directive from the Lord which has demanded response and commitment in that sacred moment. But there have also been times when I have prayed and waited for weeks and months and years.

Whatever the time-scale the primary thing is that it is the Lord's will we seek, and not some spiritual director's rubber stamp on our own! Coming to know his will is not simple, not because God is complicated but because we are. Our spiritual senses have to be trained to his direction, and that is a discipline which does not come easily to us, especially if we are used to having our own way.

God's will may be communicated directly and intuitively in the heart. It may jump at me from meditation upon the Scriptures. It may be found in the circumstances of life. It may come from the community of faith through preaching and sacrament. Or it may come in sharing with my spiritual director / soul friend.

There may be a combination of these ways with a quiet interior assurance of the Holy Spirit's confirmation. But we must be in the spiritual state of receptive openness to receive it, and a frenetic rushing around of feverish agitation will delay the process or block it completely.

In William Horwood's *Duncton Chronicles* the mole Tryfan has been left by the scribemole Boswell to a quiet contemplation of the Duncton Wood Stone which is a symbol of the dimension of religious mystery:

Tryfan looked up at it, composed himself as Boswell had taught him, and whispered, "Stone, Boswell made me a scribemole but I am not worthy. He entrusted me with the task of leading moles towards the Silence, but I have not Silence. He told me to journey, but I know not where. So now I ask for your guidance and entrust my life to you." Then he lowered his head and humbly prayed to the Stone to give them both strength and purpose . . .

Oh Stone,
In our deeds,
In our words,
In our wishes,
In our reason
And in the fulfilling of our task;
In our sleep,
In our dreams,
In our repose,
In our thoughts,
In our heart and soul always
May the wisdom of love,
And thy Silence,
Dwell always in our heart.

Oh in our heart and soul always
May thy love and thy Silence dwell.

He had a long and arduous pilgrimage to make, and this time of waiting and contemplation before the Stone brought him to a place where he could begin with sufficient light and guidance for the first part of the way.

Over 500 pages later, now a leader of many moles, more mature, grown wise in counselling others, he finds himself faced with two different ways, without knowing which to take. He turns to Mayweed, an old but canny mole who moves by intuitive wisdom rather than rational deduction, and receives an answer which rang many bells for me when I first read it:

"Mayweed . . . how *do* you choose between two routes when both seem equally attractive, or equally difficult?"

"Striving Tryfan has asked Mayweed a question which he has often thought about and will now try to answer. Humble, he learned something very useful when he was small and frightened, which Tryfan may have lost sight of in the darkness he now finds himself in: a mole faced by two choices of action may forget he always has a third, which is to do nothing. Mayweed has discovered that while he is quietly doing nothing moledom shifts and changes, and the choices he faced shift too so that one that seemed difficult becomes very easy. Mayweed suspects that Tryfan has forgotten Boswell's advice to him to do nothing and enjoy life. Mayweed humbly suggests to Tryfan that he forgets all about the choices he has to make and concentrates instead on putting one paw in front of another enjoyably. He may then find that the correct route finds *his* paws, leaving him free to snout about towards the light a bit more."

This is rare wisdom indeed, for it communicates a contemplative method which is not unreasonable but operates on a "lateral-thinking" level, defying the cold rationality of the world in which we live. "Doing nothing" is not sheer idleness. It is rather the positive and receptive stance of contemplation – the attitude which Archimedes manifested in jumping from his bath crying "*Eureka*! – I have found it!" when the breakthrough came.

In our passage from the Acts it sounds as if Paul and Timothy, neglecting this waiting upon God, were experiencing more and more frustration as they travelled through the regions of Phrygia and Galatia – and the Spirit restrained them. Then they got to Mysia and endeavoured to reach into Bithynia to preach, "but the Spirit of Jesus would not allow them to". So they went on to Troas.

They had come to a dead end, and the only guidance was negative. But in the silent hours of the night, when Paul simply let go, a vision came to him of a Macedonian calling: "Come over to Macedonia and help us!"

The text is illuminating: "After Paul had seen the vision, we got ready at once to leave for Macedonia, concluding that God had called us to preach the gospel to them." The conclusion was correct, even though it included flogging and imprisonment!

Response

* List some areas in your life where you need definite guidance and ask yourself if you are willing to accept God's will even if it conflicts with your own.

* Have you given sufficient attention to the sources of the Holy Spirit's guidance – in your own heart, in Scripture, in circumstances, in the community of faith and in spiritual direction?

* Place your desire for guidance in the context of Mayweed's counsel in today's reflection. Decide to give some time every day to silent meditation so that there is a place in your life for God's word to be heard.

> Even youths grow tired and weary,
>   and young men stumble and fall;
> but those who wait upon the Lord
>   will renew their strength.
> They will soar on wings like eagles;
>   they will run and not grow weary,
>   they will walk and not be faint.
>
>   Isaiah 40:30f.

DAY NINETEEN

Waiting

SCRIPTURE: Matthew 27:57–66. Sealing the tomb and setting a guard

Prayer

O God, Creator of heaven and earth:
As the crucified body of your dear Son rested in the tomb
waiting for the glory of the resurrection morning, so help
us to wait with him for the unfolding of your will in our
daily lives and for that final consummation of your heavenly
kingdom;
For his dear name's sake. Amen.

Reflection

It is Holy Saturday – a day of waiting. There is a quiet stillness in the orchard enclosure this morning but a feeling of calm expectation in the air.

Yesterday, Good Friday, I lettered and hung the fifteen Stations of the Cross on the plum trees which have come into glorious blossom during this Holy Week. Beginning at midday (the sixth hour) I traversed the stations with prayer, meditation and singing, accompanied by much bleating from the sheep and lambs in the surrounding fields.

Holy Saturday has always been a special day for me. There is a passivity and expectant waiting about it which is a mark of the hermit life. It is not an impatient waiting or a wanting to get out of the present but a waiting *upon* the

Lord for the unfolding of his great and mighty secret.

In this waiting process there is an acceptance of the joy and pain of the present moment. The first Holy Saturday presented no evidence or expectation of the mighty wonder which was to take place. Jesus was dead and for the disciples that was the end of all hope. They did not anticipate resurrection but were rather amazed, frightened and surprised, reacting in unbelief especially when the women witnessed to it. It is easy for us this side of Easter to wonder at the incredulity of the disciples, but what must it have been like for them?

I have spent this morning with the account of the burial of Jesus. Its importance is underlined in that all four of the evangelists record that Jesus was *really* dead, *really* buried and the tomb was *really* sealed and guarded — a fourfold witness.

There are some significant details in the texts which have given me great joy on this silent and waiting day. Putting together Matthew's account with the parallels in the other Gospels we find that Joseph of Arimathea had been a secret disciple but was now waiting for the kingdom of God with eager expectation. At this point he took courage and went in boldly to ask Pilate for the body of Jesus.

His request was granted and with Nicodemus he wrapped the body in linen with spices and laid it in Joseph's own tomb of solid rock, rolling a large stone across the entrance.

Three of the accounts mention Mary Magdalene and Mary the mother of Joses, depicting them as *following, watching, returning, preparing* and *resting* on the sabbath. The word used for watching (*theoreo*) has the sense of beholding, and the noun which is derived from it is used in the Orthodox tradition for *contemplation*. It is as if the women *gazed intently* at the tomb where Jesus was laid. And in Matthew's account where the word is not used it says: "Mary Magdalene and the other Mary were sitting there opposite the tomb."

There is a world of difference between the darkness which falls on the emtombment, sealing and guard of Matthew 27:66 and the dawning of the first day in Matthew 28:1. Something amazing has happened. We hear of an earthquake and angels, of a stone rolled away and terrified soldiers, so that it becomes impossible to put together all the accounts as they tumble over one another mingling hope, fear, unbelief and amazement. If Joseph is "waiting for the kingdom" then the King has risen from the dead and rules over death and hell.

But before all this there is Holy Saturday and the ministry of waiting. Not so much waiting *for* something but waiting *upon*, so that when the time of fruition and maturity comes we shall have been prepared in the intervening time and ready for the unfolding of God's mysterious will. For though nothing may seem to us to be happening, a great deal is going on beneath the surface of our conscious minds and within the secret counsels of God. I felt it again yesterday as I came to the fourteenth station, "The Body of Jesus is Laid in the Tomb":

> Jesus, you are really dead. Your body is cold and lifeless – and your spirit? There is a witness which says that while your body rested in the tomb your spirit traversed the dark places of Hades, bringing light and hope into the darkness. Light appeared in the dark places of the underworld as you harrowed hell and searched for our first parents to lead them up on high, leading captivity captive.
>
> So there is silence in the fragrant tomb where your body lies still and alone in strange anticipation. But in the world of spirit there is enkindled a light which shall never be quenched, and the Lord, the Spirit of Life, moves in cosmic darkness, breathing life and light and love.

There are two dimensions of activity, the earthly and the heavenly. While we live in the earthly dimension we often seem surrounded by darkness and perplexity and there is little evidence to support faith and hope. But if we wait upon the Lord in simplicity and trust, that waiting will give way to fulfilment and heaven will appear in that very place which was so dark and cold.

Since writing that last paragraph I have been into the next field gathering sticks for my Easter Fire. In the darkness before tomorrow's dawn I shall be outside my hermitage and shall kindle the new fire, saying:

> O God, through your Son you have bestowed upon your people the brightness of your light: Sanctify this new fire† and grant that in this Paschal feast we may so burn with heavenly desires, that with pure minds we may attain to the festival of everlasting light; Through Jesus Christ our Lord. Amen.

Then the Paschal Candle is lit from the fire and lifted up as I sing three times: "The Light of Christ/Thanks be to God." So shall I begin the Easter Liturgy, telling the story of salvation through the Old Testament prophecies and the Gospels with a renewal of baptismal vows and the celebration of the eucharist as the sun rises to greet the day of resurrection.

Whether the sun rises visibly or not doesn't matter because the Sun of Righteousness will have risen in the hearts of his people throughout the world.

But today I am waiting.

Response

* Have you been so much waiting *for* some future event or change of situation that you have neglected to wait *upon* the Lord in the present moment of your relationship with him?

118

* Does your life reflect more of the perplexity of the disciples before the Easter glory rather than living in the light of Jesus' new life?

* Make two columns in your journal headed *Waiting* and *Acting*. Under the first write down the values and dangers of waiting. Under the second write down the values and dangers of acting. If these two can be brought into balanced relationship then your life will neither be slothful nor hyperactive.

The Fifteenth Station

The stone had been rolled across the entrance to the tomb. Pilate's seal was set and the soldiers kept their watch. It seemed to the disciples and to the world at large that you had become a prisoner in the kingdom of the dead. It had finally come to an end.

But life began to stir within the tomb before the rising of the sun. The pure light of the Holy Spirit began to shine and your body, Lord Jesus, loosed from its imprisoning bands of myrrh and ointments, came forth in risen glory. The boundless energy of your new and immortal life burst the bands of death, rolled the stone away, blinded the soldiers and greeted the lesser sun of creation in its rising.

We remember today all the sorrows of Calvary, and feel the grief in our own hearts. But we look for the empty tomb, the glorious rising, eternal life as a present gift and grace and the life of the world to come.

"I AM he who lives and was dead, says the Lord, and behold I am alive for evermore, and have the keys of hell and of death . . ."

Remember Me

119

DAY TWENTY

Complaining

SCRIPTURE: Jonah 4:1–11. Being angry with God

Prayer

*There are times, dear Lord, when we are angry with
ourselves because our lives are not fulfilling their potential;
we are angry with our loved ones and friends because they
do not understand us; we are angry with you because you
have made us as we are.*
*Help us to pour out our complaints honestly before you,
to see clearly what it is that causes our anger to erupt and
to come to terms with the reality of our lives;*
Through Jesus Christ our Lord. Amen.

Reflection

St Jerome had a reputation for having a bad temper and some
of the old desert monks were irascible complainers. One
story goes that one of them fled into the desert so that he
would have no stupid people to blame, to grumble and to
complain about. One day he was plaiting a basket and the
material would not bend the way he wanted it. He got more
and more exasperated and at last tore it to pieces in rage
and stamped upon it. So much for the tranquillity of solitude!

It is difficult for a parish priest or clergy team when they
have to minister to people who are continually complaining,
for these people are often the same ones who complain
to their local doctor, medical panel or Parent-Teacher

Association. Nothing goes right for them, everyone opposes them and the world is set against them. And because of their constant carping their gloomy predictions are often self-fulfilling, for people begin to avoid them. Of course, sometimes it is the fault of the parish priest, the local doctor or the awkward teacher, but if there are difficult professional men and women these people will find them.

It's an old problem, because when God walked in the Garden of Eden in the cool of the say he called: "Adam, where are you?" As soon as the guilty pair turned up, he blamed her, she blamed the serpent and that's where the buck stopped (Genesis 3:8–14).

It was in the family too, because when Cain had murdered his brother and God called him to account he began to complain at the severity of the judgement (Genesis 4:8–15).

Later Esau felt that the balance was tilted against him (Genesis 27:34–36), and so it went on. The children of Israel groaned and complained quite justifiably under the tyranny of Egypt, but when God delivered them with mighty signs and wonders and set them on the road to the promised land they seemed to do nothing but complain and wish they were back under the heel of the oppressors. They grumbled against their leaders and against God (Exodus 16:7–17).

When the twelve spies were sent to reconnoitre the land, ten of them returned grumbling and pessimistic, and that set off the rest of the people. Only Caleb and Joshua saw through and over the obstacles and affirmed faith over doubt (Numbers 14:26–38). I remember the story as I sang it in Sunday school:

> Twelve spies were sent to spy in Canaan,
> Ten were bad – two were good!
> What did they see to spy in Canaan?
> Ten were bad – two were good!

> Some saw the giants tough and tall,
> Some saw the grapes in clusters fall,
> Some saw that God was in it all
> Ten were bad – two were good!

St Paul looks back upon their wanderings in the wilderness with New Testament hindsight and says in effect: "Look what happened to them – watch out and don't let it happen to you, for they are our examples" (see 1 Corinthians 10:1–11).

It was reprehensible for them to keep groaning and complaining against Moses and Aaron and finding fault with God, but it is understandable for they had a lot to put up with. But when we come to the book of Jonah and discover his problem the story becomes ludicrous.

It was not that Jonah was afraid of the heathen or that he was evading his responsibility out of cowardice or laziness. The fact was that Jonah objected to preaching to the Ninevites on religious and moral grounds. He was one of the elect people and the Ninevites were heathen and had no place among the chosen and favoured. He suspected that if he went and preached repentance to them they would possibly turn from their wickedness and God would forgive them in compassion and mercy. Even a stolid Calvinist like the famous preacher Charles Haddon Spurgeon was said to have prayed: "Lord, save the elect and elect some more."

Jonah was right, of course. God put him into the digestive system of the sea monster who vomited him out when he repented. He then had no option but to preach God's message to the Ninevites and – of course – they turned to God from their wicked ways. So we find the last chapter of Jonah opening with a sorry complaint:

> Jonah was greatly displeased and became angry. He
> prayed to the Lord, "O Lord, is this not what I said when

I was still at home? That is why I was so quick to flee to Tarshish. I knew that you are a gracious and compassionate God, slow to anger and abounding in love, a God who relents from sending calamity. Now, O Lord, take away my life, for it is better for me to die than to live."

What kind of a religion is this? Jonah complaining because the Lord was merciful! It is a sad state of affairs, but the people of God are often more judgemental among themselves and towards the world than the Lord who knows the thoughts and intents of the heart.

In the history of religion right up to the present day in certain parts of the world, zealously religious people have been and are willing to condemn, torture, kill and massacre in the name of God, justifying it by recourse to a doctrine of holy war. Jesus prophesied they would (John 16:2).

It was this kind of diabolical religion that caused James and John to want to call down fire from heaven and burn up the Samaritans because they would not give hospitality to Jesus. Some manuscripts add the rebuke that Jesus uttered: "You do not know what kind of spirit you are of, for the Son of Man did not come to destroy men's lives, but to save them" (Luke 9:51–56).

Complaining runs through the New Testament as through the Old. The religious authorities constantly murmured and complained against Jesus, often lapsing into jealousy and rage (Luke 5:17–32; 6:1–11).

But the disciples also quarrelled, disagreed, grumbled and complained. The reasons are various. There were temperamental differences (Matthew 20:24–28); objections to the hardness of the way (John 6:41–66) and differences over devotion to Jesus himself (Mark 14:3–9).

In the later New Testament Church there was a great deal of backbiting and complaining (1 Corinthians 1:10f.; 3:1–4) as well as moral and legal disputes (chs. 5, 6) and religious and theological error (11:17–22; 15:12–19). All this comes from one local church!

What then can be done with this mountain of complaint, for not all of it is peevishness and whingeing. Many people are genuinely bowed down with genuine worry, desperate loneliness, personal heartache and sorrow. There is a world full of disease, pain and loss.

In the story of Hannah in the Old Testament we are told that she was so heavy with sorrow in being childless that one day Elkanah her husband said to her: "Hannah, why are you weeping? Why don't you eat? Don't I mean more to you than ten sons?" (1 Samuel 1:8).

This brought Hannah to a place of decision. She went to the temple of the Lord at Shiloh and "poured out her complaint" to the Lord. And that's when the tide turned.

It was not an aggrieved complaining full of self-pity and accusing reproach but an opening of the heart's pain and a confession of her need. The Lord honoured such a complaint and Samuel was born to Hannah. Her gratitude was spelled out when, after he was weaned, she presented him to the Lord's service with Eli the priest at Shiloh.

Whether we are childless and desolate like Hannah, like Antony the hermit in the Egyptian desert or a contemporary Christian living out a difficult discipleship in the commercial marketplace, we can cry out to the Lord in our complaint and need, and he will hear us:

> All your anxieties, all your cares,
> Bring to the mercy-seat, leave them there;
> Never a burden that he cannot bear,
> Never a Friend like Jesus.

If you use the Psalter on a daily basis it soon becomes clear that the psalms are full of pain and sorrow as well as bursting with praise and adoration. There, more than anywhere else, we find personal and corporate outpourings of the heart's complaint to God. If we find ourselves sinking deep in the mire, groaning under intolerable burdens, infected with festering wounds or numbed and stricken to the ground, we can call to God in our perplexity. We can be honestly and violently angry, weeping and groaning in our need, having been rejected by our former friends and mocked by our enemies. And the closer we get to the real situation of deprivation and helplessness the closer we are to God. The few psalms leading up to Psalm 40 portray such distress, but that psalm is a great testimony of deliverance.

There are psalms which are full of dereliction, with no ray of light to be seen, such as Psalm 88. At the very end one is left in desolation and darkness, but the very fact that the lamentation has been poured out before the Lord gives it a place in the Psalter.

Then there are psalms which describe a similar situation but half-way through there is a sudden invasion of the power of the Holy Spirit so that the desolation is transformed into adoration (see Psalm 77). One of my favourites is Psalm 73 which goes like this:

1 God is good to the pure and holy, but I've fallen by the way and look at the state I'm in (vv. 1, 2).

2 The ungodly all around me are doing very well. They're fat and prosperous, full of sleek pride and self-confidence. They laugh at the poor and blaspheme God (vv. 3–12).

3 What was the good of all my penitence and prayer? None of it paid off. Why did I walk in the way of godliness when this is the state of things? It's all been for nothing (vv. 13–15).

4 Thinking like this I went into the house of God and the Lord shocked me to my senses. In reality they are on a slippery path, in a treacherous condition and the

ground is about to open up beneath them. Terror and destruction awaits them (vv. 16–20).

5 How stupid I've been, but you have saved me by wounding and piercing me to the heart, Lord. Thank you for bringing me low and showing me my utter need of your mercy (vv. 21, 22).

6 You've always loved me; you are always with me; you hold me tenderly to your heart. You guide me in my earthly life and will at last lead me to glory. You are the only one for me on earth or in heaven.

All else will fall away but you will remain and always love me (vv. 23–27).

7 So let me proclaim to the world the wonder of your love and witness to what you have done for me (v. 28).

Response

Comment on the following questions in your journal:

* Do you complain more than appreciate in your daily life?

* Against whom do you direct complaints – yourself, your family/friends or God?

* Can you see a value in laying your complaints honestly before God instead of covering or bottling them up and harbouring resentment?

Complaining to God in Love

One of the amazing insights of the Old Testament is the way in which the patriarch, prophet or psalmist closest to God can confront him, refusing to accept his apparent will in the name of justice, mercy or love.

Abraham could intercede for the people of Sodom on the basis of a handful of innocent people; Jacob could wrestle with God even in the perplexing confusion of darkness; Moses could argue for the sparing of Israel, accusing God of backtracking on his own promises and faithfulness.

If I feel the infinite distance between myself as sinful, mortal creature, and God as holy, immortal deity, then I fall before him in submission. But if I feel the mysterious and loving nearness of his glorious presence then I can question him, stand against him, confront him in complaint or in love. The very things which cause me to cry out in complaint, such as the holocaust of Auschwitz or the inhumanity of Ravensbruck, suddenly make me realize that I am suffering with the suffering of God – I am weeping with his tears – I am comforting him in his pain as he comforts me in my perplexity. And like Jacob wrestling with the Angel I lay hold of him in agonizing complaint and surrender to him in passive submission – and there is the mystery of healing love.

DAY TWENTY-ONE

Forgiving

SCRIPTURE: 1 Peter 2:21–25. Returning love for hatred

Prayer

Your name, O Lord, is holy, and your nature is love. We have sinned against you, against our brothers and sisters and against the deepest yearnings which you have implanted in our hearts.
In your mercy you dwell with the contrite in heart, so we ask of you true contrition, free forgiveness and the grace of the Holy Spirit, that we may walk humbly before you in mutual forgiveness and humble joy;
Through Jesus Christ our Saviour. Amen.

Reflection

One of the things I have learned in solitude is that I cannot live in integrity while harbouring hatred or an unforgiving spirit against those who have wounded me. Solitude is in some ways like a sentence of death – it wonderfully concentrates the mind. Life is too short to bear grudges and harbour malice.

In the story of Joseph it becomes clear after father Jacob's death that the brothers had failed to appreciate the fullness and depth of Joseph's forgiveness of their wickedness when they had sold him into slavery and probably death as a boy of seventeen. So they got frightened and said: "What if Joseph holds a grudge against us and pays us back for all the wrongs we did him?"

It is difficult for unforgiving people properly to receive and embrace forgiveness. So they threw themselves down before him, confessing their fears, reminding him of their father's mercy and telling him of their willingness to become his slaves.

The effect upon Joseph was that he wept because they had not fully trusted him and did not feel wholly loved and forgiven. His words provide a beautiful pattern of forgiving grace and reveal God's hidden providence in the mystery of our lives:

> "Don't be afraid . . . You intended to harm me, but God intended it for good to accomplish what is now being done, the saving of many lives. So then, don't be afraid. I will provide for you and your children." And he reassured them and spoke kindly to them. (Genesis 50:19–21)

There is immense joy in being able to forgive and a wonderful liberation in being forgiven. Out of such experiences emerge new possibilities for growth and relationship, so that even the previous hurts and wounds open up new perspectives of the healing love of God.

There is nothing so sad as a person, a group, a church or a nation that harbours malice and, instead of offering forgiveness, seeks revenge. To refuse to forgive is to allow resentment to smoulder in the breast. Even if it does not result in overt revenge or violence it will take root and spread bitterness in all other areas of a person's life. Sometimes you hear the words: "I'll forgive but I'll never forget!" Such an attitude falls short of true forgiveness which springs from mercy, humility and compassion.

I wonder if Peter had some particularly wounding experience in mind when he came to Jesus and said: "Lord, if my brother keeps on sinning against me, how many times do I have to forgive him? Seven times?" Jesus' answer of "No, not seven times, but seventy times seven" was backed up by the parable of the Unforgiving Servant (Matthew 18:21–35).

The servant in question owed his master a great amount of money and was condemned to slavery with his wife and children. After pleading with his master he was mercifully forgiven. On the way home he was met by a fellow-servant who owed him a few pounds. He grabbed the man by the throat, resisted his pleadings and threw him into prison for debt, without mercy. When his master heard the news he became justly angry and carried out the same sentence upon the merciless servant that he had imposed upon his poor fellow. How could such a forgiven man be so unforgiving? He had before him the pattern of mercy and the experience of forgiveness, but in spite of that he hardened his heart and his pleading hands became two battering fists.

If you place this parable alongside Jesus' teaching on the Lord's Prayer, certain words become significant: "Forgive us the wrong we have done, as we forgive those who have wronged us." He comments: "If you forgive others the wrongs they have done, your heavenly Father will also forgive you; but if you do not forgive others, then your Father will not forgive the wrongs that you have done" (Matthew 6:12–15 REB).

This is teaching for the child of God. The repentant sinner who comes to God is forgiven graciously and freely – and the fruit of such grace is a like spirit of forgiveness toward others. If the forgiven sinner does not forgive, likewise there is erected a barrier to further forgiveness. This means that there may be many Christians harbouring resentment and nursing revenge who themselves block God's forgiving love because of their own hardness of heart toward their brothers and sisters. This would explain much of the disunity and hypocrisy within the Church, for only where there is mercy and mutual forgiveness can charity and fellowship flourish.

Our reading today lays down the divine pattern which shows the attitude of the human Jesus returning love for hatred, not retaliating at insults, not threatening his abusers. Such silence and gentleness was not the product of cowardice or fear but the mature result of strength held in check and the overflow of his forgiving heart. "To this you were called," says the apostle, "because Christ suffered for you, leaving you an example, that you should follow in his steps."

That sounds fair enough from a pulpit or in a book of devotions where there are no enemies in sight, but it is extremely difficult and sometimes virtually impossible in an unjust and cruel world of market forces, international intrigue and senseless violence. One only has to belong to an Amnesty International group to be confronted with the personal suffering that lies behind the torture and violence practised all over the world.

Jesus was a member of an occupied and oppressed people and himself was made a victim of political and religious tyranny which at the last hounded him to a criminal's death. It was not simply the Roman soldiers and his fellow Jews who were involved in the whole pattern of injustice that led to the crucifixion. You and I were involved by our hardened hearts and unforgiving attitudes. It was sin that nailed the Saviour to the cross, and love which kept him there. When the black spiritual song asks: "Were you there when they crucified my Lord?" we have to answer: "Yes, I was there." And what do we hear as we stand by in complicity and condemnation? The amazing words: "Father, forgive them, for they do not know what they are doing."

This bewildering attitude of absolute forgiveness is repeated in the stoning of the first martyr Stephen as he prayed to the Lord Jesus to receive his spirit. Falling on his knees he cried: "Lord, do not hold this sin against them," and then he died. The primary result of such amazing love

131

and dying forgiveness was the conversion of the greatest sinner of the day, Saul of Tarsus. Tertullian wrote in later days of persecution: "The blood of the martyrs is the seed of the Church."

As someone has pointed out, the ultimate result of "an eye for an eye and a tooth for a tooth" would be a whole company of eyeless and toothless people. Violence begets violence, vendetta gives rise to vendetta, vengeance calls for more vengeance until there flow rivers of blood with no satisfaction or peace. It needs a man or woman of strong gentleness and powerful tenderness to stand where Jesus stood, to die as Jesus died, to yield his and her life for the sake of bringing an end to the violence in the name of mercy and forgiveness.

As I write there are two images in my mind. The first is the charred wooden cross on the battered altar in the ruined shell of the old cathedral in Coventry which had been bombed and gutted by German bombers, with the words written: "Father, forgive!" And this is contrasted with the statue of Sir Arthur "Bomber" Harris, architect of area bombing during the war against Hitler, calling to mind the carpet bombing of Dresden. During the 1992 London ceremony outside St Clement Dane's Church in the Strand there were nine arrests and alternating chants of "Shame" and "For he's a jolly good fellow". This statue was erected nearly fifty years after the events.

There is a cost to forgiveness – both to forgiving and to being forgiven. You will know, if you have been grievously and deliberately wounded, especially by one who had professed to be a friend, that the wound continues to bleed and remains sensitive long after the event. You will also know that if you have deeply hurt a sensitive soul who cannot or will not forgive you, it can become a source of misery or depression as your confession of guilt and penitence is not heard or thrown back in your face.

Sometimes all we can do is to forgive freely even when there is no sign of penitence or concern from the other person. Or we must admit our guilt and sorrow, knowing that forgiveness will be witheld or our plea will die on the wind.

The cost of forgiveness to the Lord Jesus was his own precious blood. It was as if he was a gambler, taking his life and throwing it for the redemption of the world. His costly sacrifice does not bring us cheap grace, but calls us to follow his pattern of forgiveness and forgiving, for this is the way of redemption.

One of the most moving settings of psalmody is Allegri's *Miserere* – Psalm 51, in which David confesses his most grievous sin against Uriah the Hittite, against Bathsheba his wife and against the child who died. But most of all against God. This psalm is so moving because it unfolds the sorrow of penitence followed by the joy of forgiveness. Together with Psalm 32, which is its companion, it presents us with a liturgy of penitence and hope in which God's tenderness and forgiving love is expressed in human emotion and yearning.

I write of penitence and forgiveness here in my hermitage today and allow my mind to be carried back, through these two psalms, into areas of deep sorrow for sin, and sensitive wounding by being hurt and grieved in heart, and I cry to the Lord in my solitude:

> Hide your face from my sins:
>   and blot out all my iniquities.
> Create in me a clean heart, O God:
>   and renew a right spirit within me.
> Do not cast me out from your presence:
>   do not take your Holy Spirit from me.
> O give me the gladness of your help again:
>   and support me with a willing spirit.

> (Psalm 51:9–12 ASB)

Response

* Record the names of those who have wounded you in any way, unconsciously, purposely or maliciously. Write the words of forgiveness you *ought* to speak even if you cannot/will not do so.

* Record the names of those whom you have wounded in any way. Write the words of confession you *ought* to make even if you cannot/will not do so.

* Hold these people and your words before God in prayer, and ask for grace to confess and to be forgiven.

He Was a Gambler Too . . .

And sitting down they watched him there,
   The soldiers did;
There while they played with dice
   He made his sacrifice,
And died upon the cross to rid
   God's world of sin.
He was a gambler too, my Christ,
   He took his life and threw
It for a world redeemed.
   And ere his agony was done
   Before the westering sun went down,
Crowning that day with its crimson crown,
   He knew that he had won.

G.A. STUDDERT KENNEDY

DAY TWENTY-TWO

Dreaming

SCRIPTURE: Genesis 37:1–11. Boyhood dreams and wide horizons

Prayer

O God of truth and vision:
You communicated with your ancient people in dreams and
visions of the night;
Open the doors of my intuition and spiritual understanding,
that I may become more aware of the realities beyond
this world which work together for good to those who
love you;
Through Jesus Christ my Lord. Amen.

Reflection

I had a dream last night. There was a perilous journey to undertake by motor cycle. Others who were making the journey were travelling by car. I wanted to keep them in sight for they seemed to know the way, but torrential rain and storm overtook us and the road became tortuous, flooded and dangerous. There was a figure of light and warmth riding pillion with me, and a quiet assurance that we were somehow protected, but it was all I could do to keep the bike on the shifting road.

I haven't worked out the whole pattern of the dream yet, as more details will come to me as I wait upon it, but I am sure it is significant for me today.

It certainly reminded me of Raymond S., one of the lads in our motor-cycling group in our late teens. I remember he rode a Matchless 350cc. One morning his married sister came over to see him. She had dreamed that he had been killed on his motor cycle and tried to persuade him not to go out on it that day. He brushed it aside, and went out – and was killed. Dreams have been very significant to me since then.

I have always had a rich and varied dream life. They have not always been symbolic, but sometimes quite specific, depicting an area of my life in which there was great joy or imminent danger, communicating positive direction or powerful warning.

There have been times when I have ignored or resisted such warning because of conceit, pride or losing face, and catastrophe has followed. And there have been times when I have listened, waited, thought about the dream, worked out its meaning and followed its counsel. Self-authenticated blessing has followed.

If a certain area is important I may have a double dream with a few nights between, and the second dream then has more details or a clearer warning or counsel. Let me illustrate this by a double dream I had just before I undertook the present prolonged period of solitude.

In *A Hidden Fire* I list the possible results of spending a time of experimental solitude as follows:

1 It could lead to a deepening appreciation of solitude and to a solitary vocation;
2 It could lead to a contemplative life with others in a kind of *lavra* or *skete*;
3 It could lead to a principle of biblical alternation – three- or six-monthly periods in silence, and the rest of the year in some apostolic and SSF work;
4 It could lead to an abandonment of solitude, returning

to active life in the Order as the primary thing;
5 It could lead to psychological disturbance.

Then I go on to make light of number 5 as a result of prolonged solitude (see pages 46–48), and say that I have a twofold safety measure against psychological imbalance or dottiness. First, I am a bit dotty already and know it, and second, I have a good sense of humour and proportion and can laugh at myself. That's well and good, and the two six-month periods of solitude went well from the point of view of the community and myself. But in March 1990, while I was preparing for what has already turned into a third year of solitude, I had two warning dreams, and with them came the awareness of their importance.

First, I dreamed of having entered into solitude and being unable to cope with it. I was surrounded and inundated by dark, cosmic powers which terrified me. Then a few nights later the dream came again, and being unable to continue, I returned to Glasshampton. When I got there I was unable to relate to people, or to minister as I used to, either in preaching or counselling. I could not correlate my thoughts or hold myself together because of the exposure in such solitude.

So, although my sense of humour has not forsaken me and I still hold it to be a measure of maturity, I do not now speak as lightly of the risks of solitude as I did formerly.

The basic meaning of a vocation to the solitary life as I understand it, is an ever-deepening experience and exposure to the divine Love. And if union with God in love is the goal, then along the way there has to be confrontation with the alienated self in which I assert my own will and independence from God. Herein is conflict.

Added to that is the spiritual combat with dark cosmic powers which is taken seriously in Scripture and in the monastic desert tradition. Thomas Merton speaks of the dread of such an expectation:

If I am what I think myself to be, and God is as I have pictured Him to be, then perhaps I could bear to risk it. But what if He should turn out to be other than I have pictured Him, and what if, in His piercing presence, whole layers of what I have known myself to be should dissolve away, and an utterly unpredictable encounter should take place? Now we begin to face human dread – the dread that cloaks the unknown encounter of death . . . We should let ourselves be brought naked and defenceless into the centre of that dread where we stand alone before God in our nothingness, without explanation, without theories, completely dependent upon His providential care, in dire need of the gift of His grace, His mercy and the light of faith.

As I reflect upon the psychological disorientation which may overtake the pseudo-mystic, I realize that the dangerous pursuit of the unregenerate self in the life of prayer is illusion, and if persisted in, may lead to madness or despair.

Reflecting upon all this today I recall a dream related to me by one of the university lecturers in 1975, when I was Anglican chaplain at Glasgow. She came to the chaplaincy and said that she had a dream which she felt was important for me.

"One of the things I appreciate about your ministry at St Mary's," she said, "is your preaching. But in my dream you went up into the pulpit one Sunday and you were struck dumb and could no longer preach." She did not know the significance of the dream, and since then I have had reason to understand it at different levels.

My double dream consisted of counsel and warning as I prepared to walk this road. It was the voice of my unconscious, informed, I believe, by the Holy Spirit of God.

There has been a revolutionary change of attitude towards dreams, and one of the main sources is the work of Carl

Jung. He has called attention to the unconscious mind which lies beneath our conscious mental responses, and which, especially through dreams, throws up images and symbols from the world of the collective unconscious.

Within and beyond the *personal unconscious* lies the mysterious dimension of the *collective unconscious* in which we share in a universal or cosmic ocean, as islands unite in the depth beneath the surface. If the door between the conscious and the unconscious is left ajar, as in sleep, then dreams can be thought of as the communicative flow of the unconscious into the conscious mind, bearing messages of grace or warning, making one aware of realities beyond the mere individual mind.

This opens up a new understanding of the dreams of the Bible. They are sometimes an invasion of intuitive awareness into the light of common day, bringing prophecies of creative joy or warning, and counsel to change one's life and attitude in the light of deeper knowledge from that mysterious world of the unconscious.

Joseph's boyhood dreams of pastoral scenes and celestial visions are both personal and cosmic in their scope, and they were relevant not only to him, but to the people of God in their wider pilgrimage. This can be understood in the light of God's providence (literally a "seeing beforehand"), communicated through dreams.

As Joseph opened up his mind and heart to such dreaming, he became open to the dreams of others like the Pharaoh's cupbearer and baker (ch. 40). Then even those of the Pharaoh himself (ch. 41), opening the door to a dramatic turn of fortune which ultimately led him to see the divine pattern retrospectively. This might have led a lesser man to discouragement and despair along the way. "Do not be distressed and do not be angry with yourselves for selling me here," he said to his brothers at the end of the story, "because it was to save lives that God sent me ahead of you"

(45:5). "You intended to harm me, but God intended it for good to accomplish what is now being done" (50:20).

In his *Jung and the Story of our Time*, Laurens van der Post tells of his own indebtedness to Jung, for he lived close to his own dreams as a child. Like Joseph, he was laughed at in his family and despised by his peers and tutors. His dreams seemed to them a deficiency in character:

> As I grew older this deficiency was seen more and more as an enemy of virtuous concentration and the seducer of will so essential for facing the facts of life which, of course, meant the facts of the physical world and the practicalities of the urgent pioneering day. That dreams in themselves were facts and whether we liked it or not were of considerable practical importance was a a notion either dismissed or instantly aborted in a ridicule of reasoning.

Fortunately he had a wise grandfather who took him on his knee one evening:

> He addressed me by my full name, as he always did when he had something of particular importance to say to me: "Laurens Jan, always remember what the Book says about Joseph and his dreams. Remember that though his brothers hated him for it, had it not been for his dreaming, they would never have found corn in Egypt and would have perished as you have heard in the great famine that was still to come."
>
> I wish I could remember the precise words of the elaboration that followed on the theme of Joseph and his dream. But I have not words so much as the feelings left in me and know little more than that over the years to come they started a process of widening comprehension.

If such thoughts are relevant and important to me as I live out my solitude and practise an openness of mind and heart

140

to my inward self and to God, they are even more important to you if you are involved in the demands of our world of increasing activity and lack of stillness.

It is only as you develop a life in which solitude and contemplation have a regular and important place that you can become open to those depths of yourself which have never yet been plumbed, and to the profound dimensions of spirit in which God communicates with the waiting heart.

Response

* Read the dream stories of Joseph in Genesis chapters 37, 40 and 41, and of the New Testament Joseph in Matthew 1:18–24 and 2:12–23.

* Comment on the relevance of those dreams in the lives of the dreamers.

* Do you believe that God speaks in such ways today? Can you recall a significant dream which seemed to indicate God's word to you?

Spiritual Solidarity and Dreams

The Bible treats humankind as if we were bound together in a psychic and spiritual solidarity, and the prophets speak out of a situation of corporate personality. This is the context in which dreams can clearly impinge on the waking world, giving guidance and direction. So much of this is lost to modern, secular men and women, though they cannot help but suspect its truth and be haunted by its possibilities.

We are like islands in the sea with a common unity in our depths. We are like trees in a forest, our common roots co-mingling in the earthy darkness. Our secular mood and our independent modernity cause loneliness, isolation and disintegration, but we long for our lost unity and yearn for a return to the community of love for which we were made. Our hearts are restless until they rest in God.

DAY TWENTY-THREE

Writing

SCRIPTURE: Luke 1:1–5. Telling the world about it

Prayer

Holy Spirit of God:
You inspired prophets and apostles to speak and write in
holy Scripture, and you constantly illumine the hearts and
minds of those who read;
Grant us a measure of inspiration and discernment in our
reading and writing, that we may discover truly who we
are and enter more fully into the nature and the love of God;
Through Jesus Christ our Lord. Amen.

Reflection

I should love to have been the man who took up his pen
in the days of the early Church and wrote: "Dear Theophilus
. . ." as St Luke was privileged to do. To pen such beautiful
and inspired writings as his Gospel and the Acts of the
Apostles was a rare honour. I believe Theophilus was more
likely to be a curious but sincere, highly placed official than
a literary device, and one of the many questions I shall ask
St Luke when we meet in heaven is how his Gospel and Acts
got into wider circulation. Imagine having written both these
documents full of fire and glory. And imagine being part
of the church fellowships which met around the eucharistic
meal while these life-giving words were read, expounded
and experienced again in the lives of the early Christians.

In these days when words are so cheap in the worlds of commerce, politics and even education, when market forces and advertising expertise further devalue the written and spoken word, it is refreshing and exciting to get back to the plain word of Scripture and be confronted with words of power and integrity.

The Gospels are so simple that a child can understand them and yet so profound and mystical that they are beyond the comprehension of a philosopher or literary critic. The Holy Spirit breathed upon the Gospel writers and they wrote under his inspiration, and the same Spirit breathes still upon the Gospel hearers and they come to faith under his illumination. There is nothing mechanistic about this for the evangelists were not word processors. The image of inspiration (*theopneustia*, literally "God-breathed," 2 Timothy 3:16) is organic, not mechanistic. It preserves the spontaneity and freedom of the writer. And such spontaneous freedom is portrayed in the reader whose mind and heart are illumined by the same Spirit:

> Here is the twofold inspiration of the Spirit: the divine power by which the word is begotten in the mind and the heart of the prophet and apostle – that is objective inspiration – and the inward illumination which takes place in the enlightened mind and heart of the believer – that is subjective inspiration. (*Praying the Bible*)

A large part of the New Testament is in the form of letters. They are apostolic epistles full of tenderness and joy, authority and warning, moral instruction and mystical revelation. We must not indiscriminately apply isolated texts to our contemporary situation without proper apostolic interpretation, for no Scripture should be privately interpreted (2 Peter 1:20). But we can see the humanity of the writer within the text. I sometimes smile when I envisage the difficulties Peter was having with some of the thornier parts of Paul's epistles when he writes: "Our dear brother Paul . . . his letters contain some things that are hard to understand, which ignorant and unstable people distort . . . to their own destruction" (2 Peter 3:15, 16).

Paul's letters to the Corinthian church had caused great rejoicing and great heartache, for in Corinth there was much to praise and much to criticize. You can feel the depth of emotion as he reflects upon the effect of his previous letter: "I wrote to you out of great distress and anguish of heart and with many tears, not to grieve you but to let you know the depth of my love for you" (2 Corinthians 2:4).

I remember preaching a series of sermons on the Letters to the Seven Churches of the Apocalypse (Revelation chapters 1–3), and catching the awe and wonder with which those churches in Asia Minor first received such blazing words of blessing, judgement, encouragement and warning. If letters are so important within the context of inspiration in the New Testament, perhaps we should reflect upon the inspirational value of the letters which we write within the relationship of friends, loved ones and fellow-believers.

I became so inundated with mail before I came to this hermitage that it proved a problem too great to resolve, so scores of unanswered letters were dealt with by a "round robin". After a warning from me, the spate of mail became hardly a trickle during the first months here, but a few people were evidently touched by the Lord to write. An evangelist friend, Eric, wrote apologetically: "This is just to let you know that I am thinking of you with much love and that I simply want to remind you that sometimes God is working in the darkness in ways that He cannot work in the light . . ." and there was enclosed a prophetic word which he felt the Lord wanted me to have:

The desert and the wilderness come before the Promised Land, but I am there in the aloneness of the desert and

I am there in the wilderness. I am not more than a pace away from you wherever you are and I choose to be with you in the wilderness because I love you and I am drawing you on to the Promised Land, to the land of joy and fulfilment, the land of peace, the land of My glory and beauty. Remember too, it is easier to stay close to Me in the desert and you are in the desert because I love you. I will be faithful to you as you will remain faithful to me. I will be faithful to you and I will grant your request, the desire of your heart.

That was a special word from the Lord for me in the darkness. Then Michael, a priest who had just left his lively church in Kidderminster to take up work as the Director of Anglican Renewal Ministries wrote: "I am not sure whether letters will get through to you, but I am writing this in the hope that this will . . ." and he went on to say:

Whilst I am greatly enjoying this work, and know it is the work to which God has called me, I do struggle with the pressure of deadlines and appointments and overfull diaries. At times of pressure, when I rush from one thing to another, I often pause and think of you and thank God that I have a brother who, on my behalf as a member of the Body of Christ, has chosen stillness and silence. I don't want to use this as a way of abandoning my responsibility to find peace and stillness and time with God, but I think you will know what I mean, and I want you to know how grateful I am to you.

Such letters as these were a gift from the Lord to me in my solitude, for although God demanded of Carlo Carretto that he destroy his address book when he went into his desert solitude, I am glad this has not been asked of me.

I have shed tears over a number of letters from dear friends who regularly pray for me and demonstrate their love, and laughed over others which clearly indicate that holiness is not a denial of a hearty sense of humour and of the ridiculous. "GO AHEAD AND RETIRE" shouted one large colourful card, "SEE IF WE CARE!" and inside there was a sprawling crowd of weeping, melancholic animals with the words: "We miss you! With love from Nick and Anne" from Structons Heath Farm, near Glasshampton.

My spiritual director and I had agreed that I should not write for publication during the first year, but I am glad that I did not lose contact with my editor. She and I have enjoyed a spiritual friendship of nearly eight years which has resulted in inspiration, creativity and great joy. None of us are able to write inspirational letters of the quality of St Paul, and we are not expected to write profoundly spiritual epistles such as Baron von Hügel wrote to his niece and to the saintly Evelyn Underhill, but we can all take up our pen and with a prayer for guidance write a simple letter of loving concern to those who may stand in need of a comforting word from the Lord.

Then what about your spiritual journal? I am assuming that you will not have got this far in your reading without attempting at least some of the "Response" exercises. Are you finding such writing of help? If you have not been used to writing a journal or diary it may be hard going. But persevere, for there is immense blessing in the ongoing use and retrospective value of such a book.

I had a letter this morning from Eileen, a Christian of only three years' standing, and her sharing of her journal is warm and perceptive, full of humorous honesty about her tribulations and wise insight about the way the Lord is delivering and leading her on.

Chris from Malvern came to see me at Glasshampton before I came away, and although he had never done such a thing before, I asked him to write up the milestones of the last ten years of his life (he was in his mid-twenties),

147

and I was overjoyed at the communicative ability which was revealed in his notebook.

As well as my own spiritual journal I keep two large scrapbooks in which I write or paste in favourite quotes from books and people, with scraps of songs, poetry, music, etc. I also have a few friends who send me typewritten quotes from their own reading which is sometimes impressive. In these ways my store builds up and it is all "grist to the mill" of reflection and meditation.

I would encourage you to do some of this as well as to reproduce important quotes in your own writing. Why not take up calligraphy or do a course in the italic hand – this makes writing sheer pleasure. To reproduce, for instance, St Teresa's prayer or a Greek or Hebrew verse using a wide italic nib and various colours enhances the value of words and writing, and imprints the text on your mind so that you picture it before you for the whole day.

I have been greatly helped by the journals of Thomas Merton, as he recorded in such books as *The Sign of Jonas* his pilgrimage of tears, doubts and anxieties as well as an evolving pilgrimage of hopes, discoveries, perplexities and joys. All this contributed to the maturity which he shared in his writings, though some of his writings (and some of mine) could not be shared because they were between God and the soul alone.

What grace and strength Anne Frank experienced in writing her diary, and what radiance has shone from it upon our lives reflecting immense courage in the midst of fear and war. The same is true of Dag Hammarskjöld's *Markings*, the Quaker George Fox's *Journal*, John Wesley's *Diary*, John Bunyan's *Grace Abounding*.

We could go back through the medieval Church to such amazing documents as Lady Julian of Norwich's *Shewings* and many others, to what is perhaps the fountainhead of journal writing – St Augustine's *Confessions*. In his

Soliloquies he relates how a voice prompted him to record his innermost thoughts so that he might more earnestly search for the truth about himself and God. The next forty years produced many thousands of pages from his hand, but none more profound and influential than the *Confessions*.

On a much lower level I picked up my first book, *A Hidden Fire*, the other evening and found myself moved to tears, not because it is great literature (I am critical of its style now), but because it does for me what Augustine's *Confessions* did for him — it records the yearnings of my heart toward God and recounts some of the experiences in which he has revealed himself lovingly, tenderly, devastatingly to my soul. I felt again in the writing itself a potential to communicate light, truth and love. And if I can persuade you, as you read these words, to record *your* story honestly, boldly and faithfully, then you will taste the fruit which has so delighted my taste, for

Those who sowed with tears
   will reap with songs of joy.
Those who go out weeping, carrying the seed,
   will come again with joy, shouldering their sheaves.
                                        (Psalm 126:5, 6)

Response

* Write into your journal the passage from St Augustine's *Confessions* beginning "Too late loved I Thee . . ." (Book X, or page 88 in *A Hidden Fire*).

* Think back to moments of light or shadow in your own experience and write up one or two of them in your journal.

* Read the following passage on keeping a journal and add one or two reasons of your own for such a practice.

Keeping a Journal

The recording of one's spiritual quest and pilgrimage, the marking of milestones, the recalling and recording of days of emptiness or splendour – all these can serve to deepen one's relationship with God in prayer and love. Such a task is like the sharing of love letters. The dimensions of the loved one's mind and heart are opened up to you, as yours are opened up to him or her. This is both a discipline and a joy, for you soon find yourself in dialogue with God as well as with your own soul. Not only will you find yourself writing truthfully about yourself at a depth unknown previously, but you will find an almost prophetic emergence of the will of God for your life as it unfolds before you in your journal. And even if this is not transparently evident, you will certainly find that the answers to some of your deepest emotional and spiritual difficulties will be implicit in the way you state the problem.

A Hidden Fire

DAY TWENTY-FOUR

Integrating

SCRIPTURE: Luke 15:11–24. "He came to himself . . ."

Prayer

Heavenly Father:
Because my heart is not set upon you
all the faculties of reason, imagination and compassion
*   have lost their centre and gone astray;*
By your Holy Spirit's indwelling
*   unite all the powers of my mind and will,*
that I may love you with an undivided heart;
Through Jesus Christ my Lord. Amen.

Reflection

Getting things together – that is what this word "integration" is all about. It can be understood in both a psychological and a spiritual sense. All my spiritual experiences have their repercussions upon my psychological and physical well-being because the Bible does not deal merely with the salvation of the soul but of the whole person, and of the person in relationship to others.

The death of parents is always a watershed in the lives of those whose relationships are good and loving. In my own case both father and mother died within three weeks of each other in 1988.

I had completed two six-month periods of solitude by 1984, and was aware that their increasing frailty meant that

I ought not to be out of reach for such a long period. I had always asked for a good death for them when the time came, and my father's increasing weakness and blindness made us see that his gentle death was right and good.

My mother was comparatively well at the time, recovering from a successful cataract operation, and my sister and I encouraged her to look forward to the spring. But within three weeks she had gone too. This caused a great deal of sorrow mingled with gratitude for them both, and helped me to see how much they had given me by simply being themselves.

My mother was a sanguine personality, much given to humorous mischief, laughter and sharing with many talkative friends and family. She was extrovert, optimistic, outgoing and never still. My father and she had shared poverty and difficult times together but she always saw the bright side, surmounted obstacles, overcame her illnesses and displayed enormous vitality and joy.

My father had a melancholic streak, little conversation and lived mainly within himself. He had few real friends and with no real opportunities had many unfulfilled hopes and untried or unsuccessful schemes. He had a profound though hidden sense of the mystery of human life which he found it difficult to articulate, and although we got on very well together it was only during the last decade of his life that he shared with me his joys and fears. There were times when we wept together during conversations in the last few years, and they remain very precious to me.

Both these mother and father poles of opposite and distinct personality traits are found in me, and a great deal of the trouble I have had over the years has been in getting these two poles together in working harmony.

My lonely and shy childhood with its solitary wandering around the coast, its private world of books and secret thoughts, were after the pattern of my father. My evangelical experience at twelve years of age threw me into a life of fellowship and witness that brought out communicative abilities and leadership qualities which brought their own demands through my teenage years. These were years of testimony, open-air proclamation, hiring a coach on a Saturday to take Rosie and her accordion and a busload of children to organized beach services after the Scripture Union pattern.

My work in hospital among the patients and my Sunday lay-preaching carried me more and more towards the ministry, first of all in the Baptist and then in the Anglican tradition.

I enjoyed my years of theological education at Cardiff, Zürich and Edinburgh, and parish ministry and university chaplaincy work in Glasgow brought me up to 1975.

All these years were after the pattern of my mother – reaching out, spontaneously inter-relating and communicating the gospel. Of course, all this was self-perpetuating, for the better I learned to communicate, the greater became the demand. I must say that one of the main things I have missed since belonging to a religious community is the loving and intimate relationship which I enjoyed as minister and parish priest. But all the while, and especially during the time in Glasgow, the deep and hidden contemplative spring was never entirely choked up – indeed, it sustained my active ministry.

But in 1975 I attended a Hermit Symposium in St David's as one of the non-hermits, and during that week I gained the perspective which put me on the road to integrating the two poles of my psychological inheritance, affirming both in the balance and harmony which led me up to the present period. Father and mother are more together than ever before!

This task of psychological integration is a spiritual work and one which every human being ought to be involved in, though the "mix" is different in every case. It is what in

Jungian terms is called *individuation*, and the quotation which ends this chapter is relevant.

This is what the prodigal son did when sitting in the pig-sty, penniless, hungry and seemingly unloved. The Greek text says literally: "But when he *came to himself*, he said . . ." Here was the beginning of getting it all together.

Note the process involved. He left home with his head held high, his pockets jingling, all the lights of freedom twinkling ahead of him, away from his father's farm, with a whole new world to explore.

The next stage is one of popularity, parties, spending and fornicating – what one of my preaching friends used to call "the high cost of low living"! He didn't have to practise asceticism and non-attachment – bankruptcy and hunger did that when the famine came. The attainment of a new perspective came to him in the pig-sty.

Reduced to a new experience of material and moral emptiness he came to himself and the road to integration and the Father's heart began. He may have strayed from his father, but his father had not strayed from him.

Response

* Is the pattern of your life one of distractions, perplexities, disintegration? Does the image which you project to the world truly reflect the inward life known only to yourself?

* If your life is to be dynamic rather than static, are you co-operating with the process and moving forward, or are you slipping back from an earlier vision or ideal which was once precious to you?

* Have you opened up your heart to another person? Do you have a confessor or spiritual counsellor so that you can avail yourself of his/her objective evaluation of your life?

154

Integrating

If you sum up what people tell you about their experiences, you can formulate it in this way: They come to themselves, they could accept themselves, they were able to become reconciled to themselves, and thus were reconciled to adverse circumstances and events. This is almost like what used to be expressed by saying: He has made his peace with God, he has sacrificed his own will, he has submitted himself to the will of God.

CARL G. JUNG

DAY TWENTY-FIVE

Dying

SCRIPTURE: Luke 23:39–49. Dying with Jesus

Prayer

*O Lord, support us all the day long of this troublous life,
until the shades lengthen, and the evening comes, the busy
world is hushed, the fever of life is over, and our work is
done. Then, Lord, in your mercy grant us safe lodging, a
holy rest, and peace at the last;
Through Jesus Christ our Lord. Amen.*

Reflection

Three weeks ago I heard from Annie's and Ken's loved
ones. They were both very ill and in an extremely frail
condition. I was already aware of Annie's condition,
feeling that the Lord was preparing her for death. I felt
very drawn to them both and began to lay aside some
of the early morning meditation time for them in their
need.

As the mornings passed I realized that they were soon
going to die and that part of my ministry for them was to
share with them in those deep places approaching death in
order for them, by God's grace, to make a good death,
crossing over into the nearer presence of the Lord.

This lasted two weeks and during that time I wrote to
Ken's wife and to Annie's daughter and granddaughter so
that when the time came for them to depart (within hours

of each other) the dying ones were prepared and so were the loved ones.

Because of this, genuine sorrow with tears could be expressed together with Christian hope because the Lord had ministered to us all. Ken had been a thoughtful agnostic, though he was willing for friends to pray for him. Eleven days before he died his wife wrote and told me that he had asked to make what he called Restitution to God and a personal commitment in baptism. In the letter his wife said: "Ken is still in this world, although only just. His body is so wasted it has the beauty and terror of a medieval crucifix." These words reminded me of the description of St Francis' body after his death:

> As for his body, it was, so to speak, transformed. For long contracted by suffering, his members had become supple like those of a child; his face was as beautiful as the face of an angel; the wound in his side seemed like a red rose; and on his flesh, but yesterday so husky, now a milky pallor shone; the Stigmata on his hands and his feet stood out like black pebbles on white marble. One would have said the Divine Crucified descended from His Cross.

As for Annie, her dying was sadness and joy for me. We have shared many hours of prayer and loving fellowship over the years. She was secretary in the church of which I had charge near Swansea, and there was a radiance and quiet joy about her faith which drew all kinds of people to her for help and counsel. I felt her prayers undergird my ministry and she has followed my pilgrimage over the years with profound understanding and love.

These have been weeks of companying with Ken and Annie, of entering into the process of their dying, and of commending them to the embrace of the God who loves them and received them at last to himself. They are now in the communion of saints in Christ and I expect to share with them in the vision of God when my time comes.

Writing like this brings back to mind the gentle death of Brother Lawrence Christopher at Glasshampton monastery some months before I came to this present solitude.

He had been ill for some months and was evidently getting weaker. The day before he died he said to me: "You won't let me go away from here, will you?" He was obliquely asking that he should die in the monastery rather than go back again to hospital. So we talked together about John who had died about a year before, and I said to him: "Lawrence, whatever happens we shall care for you as we cared for John," and assured him at that point at which he needed comfort and confirmation.

The next day he actually got up from bed and struggled to the chapel for midday prayer but afterwards was too weak to take off his habit. I got him back to bed and toward evening saw that he was getting weaker by the hour. We talked together as he lay there about resting and letting go, so that his breathing could become relaxed and easier. Before my eyes he did just that, so that I could see him let go his tension and actually co-operate with what his body was telling him.

I rang our local doctor who came after Compline when the rest of the brothers had gone to bed, though I told Brother Amos that I would come for him if I needed him.

Lawrence's blood pressure was so low that the doctor was amazed that he was still alive and we both sat with him as he slept and was evidently dying gently. At one point the doctor looked at me and nodded, and I knelt and took Lawrence's hand and said the *Nunc Dimittis*: "Lord, now let your servant depart in peace according to your word . . ."

As I finished Lawrence breathed once . . . twice . . . three times, and died. The doctor was very moved and said quietly: "I think he knew he was going." And I told him of the happenings of that day.

When the doctor had gone Brother Amos came with me to Lawrence's bedside and we said the prayers of commendation for the departing soul, including the powerful words:

Go forth upon your journey from this world, O Christian soul;

In the name of God the Father who created you. *Amen.*

In the name of Jesus Christ who suffered for you *Amen*

In the name of the Holy Spirit who strengthens you. *Amen.*

In communion with the Blessed Virgin Mary, St Francis, St Clare and with all the blessed saints, and aided by Angels and Archangels, and all the armies of the heavenly host. *Amen.*

May your portion this day be in peace, and your dwelling in the heavenly Jerusalem. *Amen.*

None of us knows much in advance the hour of our death. Indeed we would usually rather not know than be told that we have some incurable disease which leaves us with two or three months to go. We may envy Thomas Merton who finished his lecture at the monastic conference in Bangkok on 10th December 1968 and less than an hour later was lying dead under a faulty electric fan in the cottage where he was staying.

I sometimes think about my dying, for this is a very healthy thing to do, and I pray that it may be a good death. If I continue in solitude it is likely to be when no-one is around – but how can any of us know?

Some of us may look forward to leaving the body behind, especially if it has become a burden or if most of our loved ones have already gone before us. Many of the early Christians eagerly longed for martyrdom, St Francis and St

Clare among them though it was not granted to either of them.

St Paul seems to have had the right attitude when he longed for heaven and also longed to continue to serve Christ on earth:

> What shall I choose? I do not know! I am torn between the two; I desire to depart and be with Christ, which is better by far; but it is more necessary for you that I remain in the body. Convinced of this, I know that I will remain, and I will continue with all of you for our progress and joy in the faith. (Philippians 1:22–25).

He wrote that from prison and was later martyred.

Whether we live or die we are the Lord's, and nothing can ever separate us from his love. So in my hermitage I take heart from St Francis' understanding of death as his sister, who would carry him into the loving presence of God when the right time came. And you can do the same. For there is a right time and we can place ourelves confidently in the hands of our Father. As St Columba wrote:

> My destined time is fixed by Thee,
> And death doth know his hour.
> Did warriors strong around me throng,
> They could not stay his power;
> No walls of stone can man defend
> When Thou Thy messenger dost send.

There is such a thing as dying grace. When the crucified thief of our reading turned in his last suffering and called out to Jesus in repentance and faith he received assurance that he would be remembered in the Saviour's kingdom. He also entered into dying fellowship with Jesus which would never be broken, for at the last Jesus said: "Father, into your hands I commend my spirit."

Dying is a process and a moment for us all. But if we die

our little deaths to sin and selfishness in our earthly pilgrimage we shall at last hear his words of welcome: "Well done, good and faithful servant. Enter into the joy of your Lord."

Response

* Write down the names of a few loved ones or friends who have died during the last few years. During the next week use the following prayer for them.

* Write down the names of any you know who have chronic or terminal illnesses, and the name of your nearest hospice. During the week make these part of your intercessory prayers.

* Think of your part in the communion of saints and prepare for a good death.

Remember your servant N . . . . O Lord, according to the mercy you offer to all your people. Grant that increasing in knowledge and love of you, *he* may go from strength to strength in the perfect service of your heavenly kingdom, until that day when we are all united in the fullness of your love; through Jesus Christ our Lord. *Amen.*

Whoever lives and believes in Me will never die
(John 11:26)

Death is nothing at all – I have only slipped away into
    the next room.
Whatever we were to each other, that we still are.
Call me by my old familiar name,
Speak to me in the easy way you always used to.
Laugh as we always laughed at the little jokes we enjoyed
    together.

Play, smile, think of me, pray for me. ·
Let my name be the household word that it always was.
Let it be spoken without effort.
Why should I be out of your mind because I'm out of your
    sight?
I am but waiting for you, somewhere very near, just
    around the corner.
All is well.
                    Nothing is past, nothing is lost.
One brief moment and all will be as it was before, – only
    better, infinitely happier and forever –
We will all be one together with Christ.

Part III

SPIRIT

DAY TWENTY-SIX

Contemplating

SCRIPTURE: John 12:1–8. At the feet of Jesus

Prayer

Spirit of the Living God:
Fall afresh on me and let me be surrendered and pliable in
your hands;
Create in me the humility of the Lord Jesus and lead me
to adore the mystery of God the Father;
Then with holy boldness and fervour let me communicate
joy and peace to all around;
To the praise and glory of Christ. Amen.

Reflection

You quickly learn in solitude that there is a great deal of ordinariness about it. You keep to your discipline, keep yourself clean, wash your clothes, bake your bread, eat and sleep regularly, keep your grey matter active in study, do manual work, say your prayers.

There are times when I return from a walk and remove the metal bar to enter the enclosure and I am smitten with the peace and beauty of the place. Then sometimes when I am celebrating the eucharist I receive an overwhelming sense of the communion of saints. And occasionally I have wept with the sheer joy of being loved by God and by the precious experience of being here in and for him.

But there is the danger of running after spiritual "highs"

or psyching up with vigils of prayer and fasting, in excessive expectations of visions or levitations. Of course you'll have dreams and visions if you fast long enough – and receive lights and voices too – but it will all be subjective and illusory. It will be pseudo-mysticism of the kind that is sung about in Gilbert and Sullivan's *Patience*:

> You must lie upon the daisies, and discourse in
>   novel phrases of your complicated state of mind.
> The meaning doesn't matter if it's only idle chatter
>   of a transcendental kind.
>   And everyone will say
>   As you walk your mystic way,
> If this young man expresses himself in terms too
>   deep for me,
> Why, what a very singularly deep young man this
>   deep young man must be!

I'm saying two things at the same time. First, "Find God in the present and ordinary things of life and not in any special thing or experience"; and second, "Allow God to have his way with you, to take you up and fill you with unutterable glory." There is paradox here, but not contradiction.

Our business is to give ourselves to the daily disciplines of life, especially in the expressions of compassion and acts of simple humanity. At the same time we must be open to God so that he may reveal himself in ways natural and supernatural, according to his will. The whole of prayer is one, from the simple petition of the youngest child to the mystical rapture of the mature saint, and the reason we find so many grades, steps, ladders, mansions and divisions is because we think it makes it easier for us, helping us to know where we are and where we are going.

But it more often perplexes us if we try to fit ourselves into some sphere or dimension of the dark night of the soul in an effort to measure our spiritual maturity. It is like David trying to get into the armour of Saul – it simply doesn't fit!

We are temperamentally very different from one another, and though there is a broad map of the "highway of holiness", the terrain seems very different when you are on the winding path which ascends the mist-enshrouded mountain. I must find my way and you must find yours, though we must both give attention to the means of grace God has given us in his word, in his sacraments and in the world in which he manifests himself.

In order to speak more specifically about contemplation, let me make my own simple division:

1 *I say my prayers.* By this I mean the basic discipline of saying the daily office, of listening to God's word in Scripture and speaking to him in prayers of thanksgiving, petition and intercession.

2 *I make my meditation.* By this I mean the basic discipline of setting aside time in quietness to give my mind and heart to a consideration of Scripture and devotional writings, or the meditating upon some theme or topic, leading to greater appreciation of the things of God or for guidance upon the way. In this is included the expressions of gratitude and worship.

3 *I am drawn into contemplation.* Whereas in the former praying and meditating it is "I" who am active, taking the initiative in reading, thinking, praying, now I am acted upon. I am brought to the place where I am prayed through, where God breathes his Spirit upon and into me and I am caught up into some measure of the contemplation of God's glory. "We do not know how we ought to pray, but through our inarticulate groans the Spirit himself is pleading for us . . ." (Romans 8:26 REB). With what tremendous joy of

recognition did I first read Michel Quoist's responsive prayer under the heading "Lord, you have seized me". It clearly portrays the passivity I feel when God initiates the experience of love:

At times, O Lord, you steal over me irresistibly, as the ocean slowly covers the shore,
Or suddenly you seize me as the lover clasps his beloved in his arms.
And I am helpless, a prisoner, and I have to stand still.
Captivated, I hold my breath, the world fades away, you suspend time . . .
Thank you, Lord thank you!
Why me, why did you choose me?
Joy, joy, tears of joy.

Though contemplative prayer places the emphasis upon the divine initiative and properly understands that it is God who is the source and sustainer of true prayer, yet I also want to affirm that if this is to be part of our ongoing spiritual life we must be disciplined and open to such touches of God. There must be time, place, space and a regularity of waiting upon God so that when he wills he may find me there.

In my books I usually give some practical counsel of preparation in prayer (e.g., *Heaven on Earth*, pp. 25ff.), but here I shall simply indicate what happens in my present early morning period of prayer which allows an hour and a half, beginning in darkness.

I get up and dress, sometimes stepping out of the hermitage to get the feel of the morning, the sky and the surrounding quietness. Sometimes there is the hooting or screeching of owls, the occasional bleating of lambs and lowing of cattle and over the last week the gradual overtaking of the birds' dawn chorus as the mornings grow lighter.

After some gentle stretching exercises I adopt a straight-backed posture on my prayer stool – no footwear, no tight clothing. Without effort I find my body relaxed, my breathing slow, rhythmic and gentle. I then make the sign of the cross in the name of the Trinity and say: "God has sent forth the Spirit of his Son into our hearts, crying: 'Abba, Father.'" I then say the Lord's Prayer and some other memorized prayers and sing the hymn: "Father we praise you/Now the night is over . . ." This is followed either by the Jesus Prayer which leads me into silence, or I simply remain silent for the whole period of contemplative prayer.

This is not a time for prayers of petition, intercession, etc. Neither is it a time for discursive meditation on great themes or even reflection on Scripture. Nor for any cerebral thought, devotional application, appropriation of truth or consideration of theological patterns or experiences. All these have to do with "prayers and meditation" under my first two headings, and would be a hindrance during this period.

Of course one can pray with the mind, but contemplative prayer is simply "being" within the divine presence and love. It is a certain passivity, allowing God to act and move within the structure of my life, often without being able to understand or explain just what is taking place.

The result of such a period may vary greatly. The touch of God may overflow into the senses and produce profound feelings of adoration of God, compassion for fellow human beings or immense gratitude at being the object of God's loving care. This may move me to tears or even to laughter – or may bring me to a place of prolonged stillness of body and mind.

Some mornings, though, I may be moved to use part of the time, under the guidance of the Holy Spirit, to pray for particular people or events. I have described elsewhere in this book companying with dying people, simply being with them in love. At other times events of political or international importance or crisis may call for special intercession.

But usually the early morning period is for contemplative prayer – letting God have his way – allowing my time and being to be poured out before God and wasted, as Mary poured out the precious ointment upon the feet of Jesus at Bethany.

There are three accounts of this story, differing in detail, but always there is this act of abandoned adoration, the odour of which filled the whole house. There is also the anger of the disciples at the thoughtless waste of what could have been used for charitable purposes.

But Jesus allows it . . . accepts it . . . revels in it and commends the woman for her unabashed and costly love. Such is the value of love like this that he says it will go with him to his death, be remembered through all time and will be told in all the world.

There have been times when I have longed to be among unbelievers communicating the good news of Jesus with fervent zeal, or to be among believers expounding Scripture and sharing the implications of the gospel for our lives. There have been times over the last two years when I have longed for fellowship and sharing of ordinary human relations. And I have received letters from loving friends looking forward to my return from solitude or saying (carefully and apologetically) that I should be back in the turmoil of Christian ministry in these needy days.

Then I have found myself at the feet of the Lord Jesus in the darkness of the early morning, or caught up in the mingling of intercessory prayer with the political and violent dilemmas of our contemporary world, or holding before God the names and situations of people who have written for prayer in their sorrows and joys. It is a pouring out of the precious ointment upon the head and upon the feet of the Lord, recognizing that in wasting my life and time before him I am loving and adoring God incarnate in Jesus the Lord, and am serving the lost and poor of the world in the Suffering Servant.

I am writing today in the solitude of a hermitage for you who may be harassed by the numerous demands of work, home, school, hospital, family, friends, financial pressure or unemployed forced leisure. Perhaps you may be one of those who lives out their own solitude in an unvisited flat or hospital bed, longing for someone to talk to, to confide in and to love. Or you may be so consumed by the incessant demands of relationships, home and work that you long for time and space alone.

Our situation may be radically different and yet the longing in our hearts may meet in mutual recognition. Before I came here I was surrounded, even in a monastery, by continual demands on time, energy, compassion and understanding. There were times when I longed for solitude at every level. And then it came.

Who knows where you may be in two or three years' time, what relationships may be severed, what dissolution or enhancement may have taken place in your life? We only have the time and place we find ourselves in today, and God asks for this moment with whatever weariness or joy accompanies it.

Mary of Bethany knelt before the Lord Jesus; she touched his feet in humble adoration; she heard his words of gentle commendation; she felt the flowing energy that communicated itself from his loving heart.

This is the kind of contemplative spirit of which Charles Wesley writes, and which is offered to you and me if we will yield ourselves completely to him:

> God only knows the love of God:
> O that it now were shed abroad
> In this poor stony heart!

For love I sigh, for love I pine:
This only portion, Lord, be mine,
    Be mine this better part.

O that I could for ever sit
With Mary at the Master's feet!
    Be this my happy choice:
My only care, delight and bliss,
My joy, my heaven on earth, be this,
    To hear the Bridegroom's voice.

Response

* Write in your own words of the difference made in this chapter between meditation and contemplation.

* Realizing that much/most of our prayers are part of our discipline and duty, have there been times when you have felt acted upon by the Holy Spirit?

* Read through the account of the anointing of Jesus at Bethany again, and spend fifteen minutes (or more) in meditation upon its relevance to your life.

When the Spirit of God descends upon us and overshadows us with the fullness of his outpouring, then our soul overflows with a joy not to be described. For the Holy Spirit turns to joy whatever he touches . . . I tell you, when God visits us in his ineffable goodness we must be still, even from prayer. In prayer the soul utters words of speech, but when the Holy Spirit has come you must be in complete silence.

ST SERAPHIM OF SAROV

174

DAY TWENTY-SEVEN

Weeping

SCRIPTURE: John 11:28–37. Jesus weeps with compassion

Prayer

Lord Jesus Christ:
You wept at the grave of your friend Lazarus and with strong
cryings and tears spent many hours of prayer before your
Father;
Grant that my heart may be touched and my emotions
moved by the sorrow and pain of our poor world, and that
I may learn to mingle my tears and hope with those who
suffer;
For your own dear name's sake. Amen.

Reflection

One of the very positive things about the evangelical and
catholic sections of the Church is that weeping is allowed
and even encouraged because tears are a gift of God. At the
centre of such a spirituality is the penitent weeping before
the crucified Jesus. This is what drew me to the Franciscan
Ramon Lull, whose whole life can be summed up in his
words:

> When I am wholly confounded, and know not where to
> look or where to turn, then do your eyes behold me, and
> in those eyes which wept for our sins, and that heart which

175

was wounded and cleft for us do I seek and implore my salvation. And in those tears, and in that love and mercy – there do I find my health and salvation, and there alone.

The reason we can weep with sorrow or with joy before our Lord is because he wept for us. The picture of a weeping and crucified Jesus is not the image of weakness but of compassion, understanding and mercy. In our reading, when Jesus arrives at Bethany where his friend Lazarus has died, first of all he sees Mary weeping, and then he sees the people around her weeping. Entering into such mourning and sorrow the text says that he groaned in spirit and was troubled, and being led to the tomb of Lazarus we meet the shortest text in the Bible which says simply: "Jesus wept."

Jesus, weeping in the midst of his sorrowing people, portrays the only kind of God who can help us in our need. The most sublime picture of the Saviour is not the miracle-worker full of charismatic power, the authoritative teacher speaking pearls of wisdom, nor yet the contemplating guru lost in otherworldly meditation. None of these alone can enter into a compassionate understanding of the ills that weigh down our poor humanity, especially our sinfulness and mortality.

We are caught up in the finitude of our world with all its sickness and sorrow, its mourning and dying. But the wonder is greater than the sorrow – that the Christ of God entered right into the midst of it all, sharing it with us, bearing it for us and lifting us from the lowest depth to the highest height with him in Glory. I understood this as a young boy and mingled my own tears with his as I sang the children's hymn:

> It is a thing most wonderful,
>   Almost too wonderful to be,
> That God's own Son should come from heaven
>   And die to save a child like me.

And yet I know that it is true:
  He came to this poor world below,
And wept and toiled and mourned and died,
  Only because He loved us so.

Tears flow from joy as from sorrow. I can well imagine the mingling of both when the prodigal son was held within the embrace of the beloved father. My own most precious and holy moments have been those in which the gift of tears has overflowed heart and mind in loving adoration of the One who wept and suffered for me.

During the first weeks of my present solitude I entered into an experience of awe and wonder one night when the love which lies deepest in my heart was stirred by the Lord who yearns for my love as I yearn for his. I tried to describe it in my journal:

I have shed many tears since being here – for all kinds of reasons. But one evening I found myself weeping because I am loved by our Lord, and asking him not to come any nearer because I was afraid. No, that's not quite true – I did not allow myself to address him directly in prayer in case he did come any nearer. I had to keep him away because I would have disintegrated in some way. The strange thing was that I went to bed in the caravan in the darkness, and I recited audibly the way in which, through darkness, pain, self-will and hope, I had continually found my path beset by his love. Then suddenly there was this "presence" there – with me but not in me. It was longing to enfold me close and I was afraid – afraid of being smothered, I think, of almost being extinguished. In one of T.S. Eliot's poems he writes of the intolerable shirt of *fire or of fire* – that is the fire of judgement of the fire of love – the same fire. I was afraid of being wrapped in that. And I then found myself holding off such a confrontation with Love, then weeping

177

in gratitude that he allowed me to hold him off — and I wept myself to sleep . . .

Shedding tears is a way of praying, especially if you feel the mingling of God's tears with yours — just as the tears of Mary of Bethany and Lazarus's friends mingled with the tears of Jesus outside the tomb.

Madeleine L'Engle, one of my favourite children's authors, writes movingly of her husband's terminal cancer in which there is a sharing of tears and love, and the suffering does not preclude the love of God:

> Oh, my love.
> When we first learned of Hugh's cancer I was dry as the parched land suffering drought in the Southeast. Now the tears are close to the surface. For the third time this summer I come to the Psalms for the evening of the fourth day and read, "My God, my God, why have you forsaken me?" and the tears rush out silently and stream down my face. Music, too, tends to pluck at the chords of emotion. Tears are healing. I do not want to cry when I am not alone, but by myself I don't try to hold the tears back. In a sense this solitary weeping is a form of prayer.

Weeping is a form of prayer. This is the kind of weeping in which Jesus probed our finitude and mortality before the tomb of Lazarus. He understood and he stooped to share, and to bear, our suffering. Jesus wept. And in that weeping all the powers of his life-giving compassion were summoned. He brought back from death a man who had gone too far for any to hope for. "Jesus, once more deeply moved, came to the tomb. It was a cave with a stone laid across the entrance. 'Take away the stone,' he said." Martha protested because she knew that the corpse must be in a state of decomposition, but Jesus stood before her as the

Lord of life and death, and lifted up his eyes to his Father in prayer. Then:

> Jesus called in a loud voice, "Lazarus, come out!" The dead man came out, his hands and feet wrapped with strips of linen, and a cloth around his face. Jesus said to them, "Take off the grave clothes and let him go."

Tearful and fearful! Here is no machismo leader supported by the authority of the military – witness his compassion and tears. But here is no trembling wimp retreating into a sentimental and other-worldly haven – witness his confrontation with mortal agony and death.

The strange thing to some of the disciples was the way in which Jesus allowed time to pass between the receiving of Mary and Martha's call to their sick brother and his response, so that Lazarus actually died.

There was no doubt about Jesus' love for Lazarus and his sisters or about the reality and depth of the grief and tears he mingled with theirs. But they had to enter the valley of the shadow of death in naked faith before they could emerge into the glorious radiance of new life.

This is the pattern of our earthly life. The valley of the shadow has also been called the vale of tears, and every man, woman and child have their share and burden of the world's pain.

God allows it to be for a little while. But if we can catch a glimpse of the glory through our tears then what happened in Bethany when Jesus wept before the tomb of Lazarus can happen according to the measure of our own need. We must endure the groaning and travail of creation as we share in the pain and compassion of our common humanity, but we are invited to share in the beginnings of a world redeemed where the prophecy will at last be fulfilled:

Now the dwelling of God is with mankind, and he will

live with them. They will be his people and God himself
will be with them and be their God. He will wipe every
tear from their eyes. There will be no more death or
mourning or crying or pain, for the old order of things
has passed away. (Revelation 21:3f)

Response

* Write down occasions when you wept 1) in mourning;
  2) in sharing; 3) in love.

* If you have never wept in adulthood, do you think that
  1) you may be deficient in your emotional life, or 2)
  shedding tears is not your style? Add some comments
  to justify your conclusion.

* Make this whole area a matter of prayer, asking for
  deliverance from weak sentimentalism and (if you can)
  for the gift of tears.

The Gift of Tears

The fruits of the inner man begin only with the shedding
of tears. When you reach the place of tears, then know that
your spirit has come out from the prison of this world and
has set its foot upon the path which leads towards the New
Age. Your spirit begins at this moment to breathe the
wonderful air which is there, and the moment for the birth
of the spiritual child is now at hand, and the travail of
childbirth becomes intense. Grace, the common mother of
us all, makes haste to give birth mystically to the soul, God's
image, bringing it forth into the light of the Age to come.
And when the time for the birth has arrived, the intellect
begins to sense something of the things of that other world
– as a faint perfume, or as the breath of life which a new-
born child receives into its bodily frame. But we are not

accustomed to such an experience and, finding it hard to endure, our body is suddenly overcome by a weeping mingled with joy.

ISAAC THE SYRIAN

DAY TWENTY-EIGHT

Laughing

SCRIPTURE: Acts 16:16–40. Joy and singing at midnight

Prayer

*You are the source of all joy and humour, Lord, and yours
are the springs of spontaneity and playfulness;
Set our spirits free that we may join in the laughter of the
wind, sea and sky;
Enable us to communicate joy to those in sorrow and
despair, and gently to bring out the humour and laughter
that lie hidden in their hearts;
Through Jesus Christ our Lord. Amen.*

Reflection

There is such a thing as holy laughter. It arises from at least
three sources. The first is the realization of one's place in
the whole cosmic dance, as part of the great game of creation
and of the exuberant playfulness of being alive. It is
manifested especially in the springtime when the sap has
risen, the lambs are leaping and the hares are dancing. The
sheer joy of life, of being young, of being human, of being
in love, of being part of the whole natural process – this
gives rise to spontaneous joy and laughter and this laughter
has the nature of glee, of celebration and of sharing. There
is no spitefulness or cynicism about it. It is holy because it
belongs to the innocence of creation responding to its
Creator.

There is the other side to that, of course, which is the poetic melancholy and dying of the autumn which expresses the yearning of finite creation for immortality, but let's stay with laughter and joy for the present.

Secondly, laughter may arise from the sheer ridiculousness and absurdity of human claims when we take ourselves too seriously and strut about in pompous fashion in uniforms and ritual garments full of self-importance and conceit.

When the little boy in the crowd sees clearly that the emperor is naked and shouts the fact with glee, then the people's imagination is freed from the illusion of robes too wonderful for their unworthy eyes, and they begin to laugh until tears are streaming down their cheeks. The ill-proportioned and pot-bellied emperor is carrying himself with earnest mien – and then the balloon is pricked and the illusion shattered. The only human response to the absurdity of the situation is good, open, honest belly-laughter, and everyone joins in – except, perhaps, the emperor!

Governments and religions need to laugh at themselves – it shows some humility and saves them from fanaticism. If politicians, military top-brass, bishops, clergy and house church elders could laugh at their own importance and ridiculous posturing the world would be a little more human and a little more humble as well as a little more humorous.

The third source of holy laughter is the sheer, infectious joy of being God-intoxicated. Of course the world counts this as foolishness, but the foolishness of God is wiser than human wisdom and the wisdom of God is counted foolish by the carnal and materialistic.

The thirteenth-century Franciscan friar Jacopone of Todi was firmly in the tradition of being drunk with the love and compassion of Christ. The rapturous adoration and emotional exaltation that often overwhelmed him he called *Jubilus*, and he writes of it in stanzas like these:

The *Jubilus* in fire awakes
    And straight the man must sing and pray;
His tongue in childish stammering shakes,
    He knows not what his lips may say,
    He cannot quench or hide away
      That sweetness pure and infinite.

The *Jubilus* in flame is lit,
    And straight the man must shout and sing;
So close to Love his heart is knit,
    He scarce can bear the burning sting;
    His clamour and his cries must ring,
      And shame for ever take to flight.

The *Jubilus* enslaves man's heart,
    – A love-bewildered prisoner –
And see! his neighbours stand apart,
    And mock the senseless chatterer;
    They think his speech a foolish blur,
      A shadow on his spirit's light.

There are many passages of Scripture which make me laugh and sing for sheer joy. Take, for instance, that lyrical passage of praise for Jesus the Saviour in the first letter of St Peter which enjoins joy through suffering because Jesus has conquered death and hell and then continues:

> Though you have not seen him, you love him; and even though you do not see him now, you believe in him and are filled with an inexpressible and glorious joy, for you are receiving the goal of our faith, the salvation of your souls.

The response of laughter to this passage is an expression of the unbounded hilarity with which such good gospel news is received. It is holy because it has to do with wholeness, with a salvation which is physical as well as psychological and spiritual.

The above quotation is from a context dealing with this good news in the middle of trials and persecution, showing that such laughing, singing and praying are not at all incompatible with the various trials with which we are confronted in our earthly lives. The Scripture for today's theme also makes this very clear. You can imagine the laughter which Paul and Silas shared as they looked back upon the events which led to their shackling and imprisonment. They were wrongly accused, dragged before magistrates, stripped, severely flogged, thrown into an inner cell for complete security and chained to the wall with their feet fastened between heavy blocks of wood.

About midnight they could contain the glory no longer. Paul and Silas began praying, praising and singing loudly (they couldn't dance because of the chains and stocks!). Perhaps they were even singing Psalm 126:

> When the Lord restored the fortunes of Zion,
>   then were we like those who dream.
> Then was our mouth filled with laughter,
>   and our tongue with shouts of joy.
>
> (vv. 1–2 RSV)

Anyway, the result of such ebullient praise was the shaking of the foundations as an earthquake caused the prison, the prisoners and the jailer to tremble – with joy and with fear. The prisoners were liberated, the jailer and his family were saved and God was glorified. I'm sure laughter mingled with the rejoicing.

Of course you have to be a bit dotty to enter into the exuberance of such an experience. My own Franciscan tradition is full of laughter and folly, as I've already mentioned. But even earlier, in the eleventh-century hermit tradition of Peter Damian's *Life of St Romuald* we find a man whose life in the Spirit often caused him to dissolve in tears and burning with the ardour of love for God.

There are two particular ways in which he illustrates holy laughter. He is a warm-hearted and humorous hermit and his spiritual warfare involves irony and laughter against the evil spirits who threaten him:

> Look, I'm ready, come on; let's see your power, if that's what it is! Or are you really powerless? Are you already defeated, don't you have some secret weapon to bring out against God's little servant?

Martin Luther later said that the devil should be laughed at, so both he and St Romuald were obeying the injunction of the apostles: "Resist the devil and he will flee from you" (James 4:7; 1 Peter 5:9).

The second way in which St Romuald illustrates holy laughter is when he uses it in conjunction with compassion towards sinners in the context of a playful sense of fun. A thief has broken into Brother Gregory's cell:

> In his mirth the holy man said, "Brethren, I just do not know what to do with such a wicked man. Shall we tear out his eyes? But then he won't be able to see. Shall we cut off his hand? But then he won't work any more and will probably die of hunger. Shall we chop off his foot? Then he couldn't walk. No, take him inside, and give him some food, so that meanwhile we can work out what to do with him." And so the holy man, exulting in the Lord, fed the thief and then humbly chided him and admonished him with sweet words, letting him return home in peace.

There is a kind of laughter which is not holy and is well illustrated in the Bible. It is the laughter of unbelief. Abraham and Sarah laugh in the face of God's promise of a child (Genesis 17:17; 18:12), but this is gloriously reversed when the child is born and they both break into godly laughter and call the child Isaac which means "he laughs" (Genesis 21:6).

Unholy laughter is that of derision when your enemies have you just where they want you (Psalm 80:6) or the laughter of cynicism when your best efforts are rubbished by onlookers (Nehemiah 2:19).

Jesus was faced with scornful laughter when he went to heal Jairus' daughter (Mark 5:40), but he said that all this unholy laughter would be turned into mourning when the day of God's wisdom would come (Luke 6:20–26).

Holy laughter is also an antidote to fear, for in being able to step back from our own narrow and provincial situation of seriousness and fear a kind of cosmic perspective of eternity broadens our view and widens our horizons. A freedom is experienced in which God's view of things comes to our aid and our petty fears are caught up into the wider view of God's kingdom.

Immediate radio and satellite TV present us with the world's suffering as it happens. One of the results of this is to plunge many people into an acute form of depression which paralyses good intention and action, and can lead into a chronic depression which may end in despair.

Here is all the more reason to allow the gospel to sustain joy and hope in the middle of political and international darkness so that creativity and compassionate action is stimulated. Cynicism and despair are the counsels of the devil. Laughter, joy and hope are the fruits of the love of God.

Rabbi Lionel Blue illustrates this in one of his funny Jewish stories. A rabbi had fallen down a rock crevice while amateur rock-climbing, and found himself hanging on to a sapling growing from the rock face, precariously perched over a sheer drop. He looked up to heaven.

"Is there anybody there?" he cried. "Please help me." A comforting voice responded: "Trust me, my son. Relax and

let go your hold, for underneath are my everlasting arms."
Silence. After a few moments the rabbi called out again: "Is
there anybody else there?"

Response

* Write down the names of three friends who have a sense
  of humour, and three who do not.

* Of the first three, would you appreciate them more or
  less if they had no sense of humour? Of the second three
  would you appreciate them more or less if they had a
  sense of humour?

* Does this exercise say more about you or them? Would
  you say that laughter and humour indicate maturity or
  childishness? Why? Put these questions in the context of
  our reading today and meditate upon it for at least fifteen
  minutes.

If there is play, humour, laughter between brothers and
sisters, then life will flow and tears are more easily shared
in times of pain and suffering. An inability to share joy
inhibits the sharing involved in sympathy and compassion,
and a humourless person is often lacking in other dimensions
of his or her emotional life. These words need to be said
because there is a type of person who cannot celebrate the
sheer joy of creation and redemption, and nevertheless is
incurably religious. Such people are found in all parts of
the Church and are one of the main reasons why ordinary
human beings with rich emotional lives are turned away
from the life of faith. Of course you don't have to be overtly
laughing and certainly not putting on the mask of an
evangelical or liturgical smile all the time (Lord, save us!),
but joy and humour should be mingled with the whole

spiritual and human quest . . . In such a situation humour sometimes produces laughter, but more often a quiet smile of complicity and understanding.

Deeper Into God

DAY TWENTY-NINE

Empathizing

SCRIPTURE: Leviticus 25:8–13 and 39–43. The Year of
Jubilee

Prayer

Compassionate and Loving Father:
May all those who are now exiled one day return home;
may those who have wandered in rebellion, sinfulness and
  neglect feel the need of their Father's love;
may those who have been taken captive find in you their
  hope;
and may the sharing of our compassion and the joyfulness
  of our welcome put to flight the wasted years of pain;
Through Jesus Christ our Lord. Amen.

Reflection

Empathy is understanding, sharing, bearing another's
burden or joy. It is being with the man whose wife suffers
from Alzheimer's disease and does not know him though
he nurses her day and night; it is officiating (or simply
rejoicing) at the wedding of a young couple who are simply
and clearly so much in love; it is holding the hand of
a ten-year-old little girl who has a brain tumour and is
now blind.

Sometimes it is being drawn very close to them in
conscious sharing and sometimes it is the ministry of
profound prayer in geographical separation. But always it

is entering in, feeling their emptiness and pain or being elated by their happiness and peace.

When Terry Waite was at last released in November 1991 I was not alone in experiencing the glory of that day, and although some time has elapsed, I want to share with you the way I felt then, communicating the gratitude and relief of empathy after years of patient and yearning prayer.

I write on a grey day but a splendid day. It has rained all night and at 5.45 a.m. going up to do the chickens it was the darkest and muddiest day for weeks. It continues to pour with rain and the caravan is trembling in the wind.

But it is a splendid, a glorious day because Terry Waite was released last evening after 1763 days of captivity. He and Tom Sutherland are free, and are talking about the release of hostage Terry Anderson and the other Americans who are left. I have pictures of Brian Keenan, John McCarthy, Jackie Mann and Terry Waite on my wall and they have been woven into my crying and praying through all the months of my solitude. And now they are all free!

I know it is not just *my* prayer, but my prayers have been part of the warp and woof of the pattern of yearning, longing, sympathy, compassion, empathy. I've been considering those words: *sym-pathos, em-pathos, com-passio* − all entering into, taking upon/within oneself the pain, the suffering, the feeling, the yearning for freedom, for release, for healing. This is *my* work, *my* pain, *my* glory. But it is not just *mine* but everyone's. I was moved in reading Albert Einstein's words written in the *New York Post* in 1972:

192

A human being is a part of the whole, called by us the "Universe", a part limited in time and space. He experiences himself, his thoughts and feelings as something separated from the rest — a kind of optical delusion of his consciousness. This delusion is a kind of prison for us, restricting us to our personal desires and to affection for a few persons nearest to us. Our task must be to free ourselves from this prison by widening our circle of compassion to embrace all living creatures and the whole of nature in its beauty. Nobody is able to achieve this completely, but the striving for such achievement is in itself a part of the liberation and a foundation for inner security.

". . . widening our circle of compassion to embrace all living creatures and the whole of nature in its beauty." I would add: "and its suffering".

The wind is still high but the rain has stopped at last and I feel the need to walk down my neighbouring field to the brook at the bottom which this month has swelled to a wider and deeper stream. I'll finish these words when I return . . .

. . . Oh yes, the ground is soggy beneath my feet, the wind lashes the branches above my head, causing droplets of water to shower me, and the swirling waters of the stream are carrying sodden leaves and small clods of earth in its onward rush on this darkening late November afternoon.

And I rejoice and sing for Terry Waite, and through him for all those who have experienced liberation, freedom, release at any level in this poor November world of ours. And the rain comes again — and the wind — and darkness overtakes the world. But nothing can extinguish the light which shines on in the darkness, for the darkness cannot overcome it.

Dr Robert Runcie and Archbishop George Carey met Terry in the 'plane last evening. The weather was too wild to meet outside. They represented the Church catholic, and the bells of the London churches were ringing. I did my own charismatic dance outside my hermitage, for we are all in this together.

It was in the loneliness of his prison that Terry remembered what he had said previously in case he should be taken hostage: "No ransom is to be paid and no exchange made . . ." The Lord undergirded his courage and strength in darkness and captivity. When Sue Lawley asked him about his feelings on *Desert Island Discs* he told her that in that situation he had determined that there should be "no self-pity, no regret and no sentimentality".

So when that glorious day of liberation came he must have felt like the slaves in our reading where, in the Year of Jubilee, the prison doors were opened, the captives were set free and the land rang with the singing of the songs of freedom.

Wistfully I look for that spiritual Year of Jubilee when all the exiles return home to the Father, when swords shall be beaten into ploughshares and spears into pruninghooks and when the cattle and the people shall no longer tremble as they did today when the low-flying military planes screech and roar over the lovely hills of Wales. And the Father's heart shall rejoice.

Response

Comment upon the following questions in your journal:

* Can you see a value in keeping before you the names of prominent Christians, politicians, hostages, oppressors, victims, etc., at present in the media, for purposes of intercession?

Empathizing

* Do you spend any time reflecting upon the joys and sorrows of fellow human beings throughout the world? And do you spend any time *being* with them — in visiting or prayer?

* What practical ways can you see of fulfilling the Einstein quotation in this chapter? What about letters to prisoners of conscience encouraged by Amnesty International?

Entering into Compassion

Many people have never experienced real compassion or empathy. In order to do so you must be capable of *passion* — a suffering in ecstasy or despair — and most of us are afraid of that. But Jesus was not. He entered into profound pain and suffering. He was exalted to sublime glory and ecstasy. And all for us.

If we allow ourselves to be truly incorporated into Christ and allow Christ to indwell our inmost hearts, then we shall be capable of compassion, and we shall empathize with the poor and despised, with the joyful and ecstatic. And all for him.

DAY THIRTY

Doubting

SCRIPTURE: Luke 7:18–23. Who are you and who am I?

Prayer

Sometimes, our Father, we are beset by doubts and questionings which arise from unbelief and the inability of the unregenerate heart to understand the revelation of your love. At such times, forgive and enlighten us in truth. Sometimes, our Father, we are afraid to question teachings and doctrines that are contrary to what we know of love and truth in our experience. At such times, let doubt be a positive instrument of your discipline and lead us gently into an examination of what has been handed down to us by authority, in honesty and integrity.
But in all things, our Father, keep us within the fellowship of your Church, obedient to the life and teaching of our Lord Jesus Christ who is the Way, the Truth and the Life. Amen.

Reflection

From a child John the Baptist lived in the desert, preparing for his unique mission as the forerunner of the Messiah, the voice that cried in the wilderness. When the time came, after four hundred years of prophetic silence in Israel, he preached a powerful and charismatic message of repentance, baptism and preparation for the coming of the Christ.

There was no doubt in his mind, no ambiguity in his

preaching, no compromise in his witness. But now all that was in the past.

As a result of his denunciation of Herod Antipas for his immoral marriage John was imprisoned in the fortress of Machaerus near the Dead Sea. Incarcerated, cut off from light and freedom, attacked by doubts and fears, he sends two of his disciples to ask Jesus: "Are you the one who was to come, or should we expect someone else?"

Gone seems to be his former assurance, boldness and clarity of mind. Their place is taken by pain, anguish and distress. The problem of identity which clouds his vision concerns the identity of the Christ as well as his own self-doubt.

His circumstances only compound the problem. The dank loneliness and isolation of his cell becomes interiorized and the dividing-line between objective truth and subjective vision becomes blurred as he doubts the reality of both.

This is one kind of doubt which is possible for any of us, and let those who think they stand take heed lest they fall! John had not denied his vision or sinned against grace. His incarceration was itself a result of his courage and faithfulness. But the physical privation of imprisonment, together with the mental fatigue of a demanding ministry and the draining of spiritual energy, had brought about a reaction which seemed to indicate a collapse of faith.

I believe this was God's way of bringing John into a completely new understanding of the nature and content of Jesus' message which was far more revolutionary than he had ever envisaged – a revolution of love. And as such, it was a preparation for John's martyrdom.

John the Baptist did not belong to the guerrilla movement which sought to bring in the kingdom by military might and force the messiah to show his hand. But he did believe that the messiah would rule from Jerusalem, the city of David, and would throw off the Roman yoke of occupation. This meant political revolution, and the only means of such revolution was some kind of military confrontation. Hence the distressing ambiguity and doubt inherent in the question asked of Jesus.

But see what Jesus does. He reorientates such nationalistic and patriotic thinking away from a military messiah and sends to John a completely new agenda of redemption and salvation through compassion and mercy:

> Go back and report to John what you have seen and heard: The blind receive sight, the lame walk, those who have leprosy are cured, the deaf hear, the dead are raised, and the good news is preached to the poor. Blessed is the man who does not fall away on my account.

Another rendering of the last sentence is: "Happy are those who have no doubts about me." But the Greek text actually says: "Blessed is the one who is not scandalized by me." And the word *skandalizo* is the one St Paul uses of the crucified Jesus (1 Corinthians 1:23f.). It is as if Jesus is speaking of their common suffering which would bring them into the kingdom of peace.

We are not told how John received this message or how he worked it out, but here we have a pattern of the way in which doubt leads to a collapse of what had been and provides a spiritual exploration and understanding of a new way. John's inability to match the old understanding of a nationalistic messiah with who Jesus was and what he was preaching caused doubt and perplexity – yet led to a revolution of faith and a renewal of vision.

This has been part of my own spiritual journey. My early teaching was a fundamentalist dispensationalism which justified all the sanguine wars of massacre, pillage and extermination in parts of the Old Testament as the will of God. Only this week I heard a clergyman on the radio maintain that AIDS was God's punishment for sin and prophesied in Deuteronomy 28:20–22! This was formerly taught in relation to the Black Death, the Plague – indeed any pestilence that destroyed populations in epidemic proportions.

Dispensationalism also taught a view of Christ's Second Advent in which there was to be a literal bloody Battle of Armageddon in which the Suffering Servant would revert to a Conquering Hero of messianic proportions, pouring out plagues and misery upon the world.

It was clear, when the Gulf War became a terrible reality, that all these teachings were alive in forms of fundamentalist evangelicalism. I was so glad to receive the magazine of one of our foremost evangelical Bible colleges which published timely theological articles on Old Testament prophecy with biblical exposition which was gospel-centred with a radical perspective on Jesus as reconciling Saviour and not as military messiah.

For me, doubt was the beginning of this theological revolution. I needed the courage to reject an understanding of the nature of God which was that of a tyrannical despot who fills the world with plague and violence and not simply condones but commands wholesale extermination of Israel's enemies (who were also his creation) to his praise and glory!

Many people who are brought up under such a religion of terror and guilt either throw it completely overboard (as some of my friends did), or through positive and creative doubt break through into an understanding as radically different as that of the disciples after the resurrection of Jesus.

I remember first reading the Catholic theologian Charles Davies' book *A Question of Conscience*, which recorded his pilgrimage of doubt, conflict and reaffirmation. For him it was necessary to break away from the ecclesiastical domination of bondage which was his experience, in order to affirm the spiritual reality of the Church of Christ. He says that in so doing he felt as if he was rejoining the human race, and goes on to say:

> Happiness, I suggest, does not lie in a security gained by anchoring the mind in fixed formulations and resisting the tidal wave of human questioning, but in allowing oneself to be carried forward towards new horizons, confident in the guidance of the Spirit as manifested in the creative thinking of Christians in communication with one another.

I am not writing against either the evangelical or catholic sections of the Church but pointing out the fallibility and sinfulness of any section of the professing Church which puts its trust in the power of arms, money, domination or religious doctrines which betray the reconciling and redeeming power of Jesus Christ the Saviour.

We must welcome creative doubt which undermines such corrupt religion, and remember that all the main religions of our world are corrupt in various ways but that they all have a faithful remnant of people who seek in mind and heart to live close to the revelation of God's love.

The sense of release and freedom some people experience when they are able to question and reject pseudo-religion is quite exhilarating. In Mary Hocking's novel *Good Daughters*, teenage Alice has been exposed to strict Methodist religion with which she has been struggling for some time. The crunch came when Katia, her Russian-Jewish friend who lived next door, went off on a visit to Germany (1930s) and got caught up in anti-Semitic violence, disappearing without trace.

Alice expected God to save and bring her home. At the beginning of a week away from home she made a desperate act of faith and prayer, expecting to find Katia there when she returned.

Returning home she realized that this God had done nothing. Suddenly, reaction set in and the whole theology of childhood collapsed. She ran upstairs and exploded in tears of anger, words of hate and a denial of God:

She hated each and every aspect of Him; He had been the most negative influence in her life, and although she could not express this in words it was all there in her cry of hate. "I hate you! I shall never speak to you again!" And – which was more – she told Him He didn't exist. And behold, He didn't! He was gone, just as if she had opened a cupboard and given everything a good shake and a moth had flown out. She was free of Him!

The freedom was tremendous, she felt it travel along her spine, her head was spinning with it; she went to the window and seemed to be walking on air. There was nothing inside her, she had breathed Him out of her, emptied herself of Him. She felt cleansed.

But it didn't end there. For suddenly, God took the place of god, and it was just as dramatic:

She had thrown down a challenge which had been taken up. Or was it she who had been challenged? Was this what others meant when they talked about being saved, called? She didn't think it could be. They made it sound so comforting, as though something had been settled once for all. She wanted *that* for herself, had prayed for it, had tried to do the things which seemed to work for other people, but nothing had happened. She had been passed by. So why now, when she didn't expect it, had certainly done nothing to deserve it? Why *this*?

It was as if Alice had had a vision and something had taken place within her by an act of grace. Her orientation towards God seemed now to operate in a new dimension:

From now on she would speak to God hesitantly, inter-mittently, reluctantly, fervently she would speak her anger, despair, her joy and adoration, grief and longing: the dialogue, the wrestling, the coming and going of love and hope, the ebb and flow of belief, the finding and the losing of the threads in the pattern, the exhilaration of success and the bitterness of failed expectations; these would not cease. And there would always be God, the God of now and the God beyond the God of now; unattainable, inescapable, unpredictable, suffering from a fundamental inability to obey man's rules, who might demand of one person crucifixion, and of another that she accept the gift of life.

The place where Alice's doubt in the God of her old religion appeared was in a world preparing for war, in which anti-Semitism was one of the symptoms of coming violence and inhuman cruelty and where a heartfelt petition had been made to this God. This doubt brought on the crisis and the crisis had produced the vision, the breakthrough, the new awareness of God beyond God which was grounded in experience as a gift of grace.

This is the God with whom we are confronted, with whom, like Jacob, we must wrestle in conflict and perplexity (Genesis 32:22–32). As Jacob wrestled with such a God it involved identity – the name and nature of God and the changing of Jacob's name. None of this is accomplished without pain and struggle. For Jacob it was the dislocation of his hip joint – and he went lame for the rest of his life.

Believing in God is not only an act of faith responding in love. It is also a continuing journey of creative doubt. We have fabricated a mental image of God. But he is beyond any conception we may have constructed, and by creative doubt our mental image is demolished and a new understanding, a new experience and vision is born within us by the Holy Spirit. And the process continues.

Miguel de Unamuno, the Spanish philosopher, struggled

202

with belief in God over his lifetime and his struggle is communicated in the classic *The Tragic Sense of Life*. Perhaps our understanding of the reality of God should be compared with his words which conclude this chapter.

Response

* List any doctrines of the Christian faith which have raised doubt and perplexity in your mind.

* Have you found yourself doubting the existence, the power or the love of God in any particular circumstance of your life?

* Can you believe that doubt may be a positive and creative experience in the exploration of the life of faith? In the light of 1) and 2) above, how may this apply to you?

To Believe in God

Those who believe they believe in God, but without passion in the heart, without anguish of mind, without uncertainty, without doubt, and even at times without despair, believe only in the idea of God, and not in God Himself.

MIGUEL DE UNAMUNO

DAY THIRTY-ONE

Sorrowing

SCRIPTURE: Matthew 2:13–23. Herod's massacre of the
Holy Innocents

Prayer

Heavenly Father:
Your heart is full of mercy and compassion. As a father you
protect and strengthen me; as a mother you sustain and
enfold me to your heart.
In all the personal and communal sorrows of my life help
me to discern the close-knit web of compassion and care
that surrounds me, and pour into my wounds the balm and
healing of your Holy Spirit;
Through Jesus Christ my Lord. Amen.

Reflection

Joy and sorrow interwoven reflect human existence and are
part of life. We see these themes illustrated in our prayers
and reading today. The death of a single child by sickness
or accident calls forth our deepest sympathy. The abuse and
death of a child by cruelty, intimidation and violence plunges
us into perplexity and sorrow. The account of Herod's
murder of the infants reminds me of the Aberfan disaster
of 1966 when over a hundred children were killed in the
tip subsidence which engulfed their school. The church was
also affected and the new building which was erected was
dedicated appropriately to the Holy Innocents. I remember

preaching there just afterwards and from the pulpit being able to see the glistening white gravestones on the hillside. Such social and community darkness involves and affects us all.

One Sunday recently was a dark day such as visits me from time to time. The colour and texture of the sorrow of such days differs greatly, and my response changes greatly, yet such days are part of the pattern. I don't mean part of the pattern merely of *my* life but of human life.

I am grateful for my evangelical grounding in the gospel but am suspicious of the kind of Christian who claims constant and continuous happy assurance, victorious sanctified living, free from doubts, conflicts and questioning. I wonder how a Christian can live in a world like this and *not* enter into much and deep sorrow. Unless this is so, he or she cannot be a true follower of the One who was "a man of sorrows and acquainted with grief". How can any Christian, indeed any human being, live as if they were not part of our poor world?

I don't mean that we must allow ourselves to be submerged in the pain and sorrow of it all, but part of our humanity is to enter into, share part of, participate in, the common sorrows of our human lot. Then not to stop there but to go on and positively enter into and redeem those areas of our own and others' sadness. If we could see it, this is the privilege of every man and woman of integrity, and certainly of the Christian.

The difficulty is often to discern the difference between simply our own sadness and grief and that which belongs to friends, to the community or to the world at large, in order that we may act redemptively in prayer on their behalf. Of course there is sometimes no way of separating our own from those wider concerns. I believe, for instance, that during my six months' solitude on the Lleyn Peninsula in 1983/4 I entered not only into some of the world's sorrow in redemptive prayer, but also into the beginnings of conflict with dark powers.

My own psychological maturity and growth were involved too, and the months of winter there, with violent storms, crashing seas and driving wind and rain on an exposed mountain, all contributed to the darkness. There was glory too, of course, and rising and setting suns which took my breath away as I sometimes danced (or jogged) around the mountain and along the sandy shore.

But there are ways of sometimes differentiating between my own sorrow and that which I share and work through with a brother or sister, with the community or the world. On this particular Sunday, for instance, I found that soon after waking I began to feel a cloud of darkness. It was oppressive and there was no obvious reason for its appearance.

I went up and did the chickens, returning to my usual Sunday morning of eucharist and intercession for all who remember me in prayer and for the special needs of those who have written with requests. It was like swimming in molasses, and I could feel no joy or light during the morning.

Sometimes when this sort of darkness overtakes me I feel a listlessness and inability to write or record my diary, as if the paralysis which arrests my prayers invades also any creative movement. Occasionally this is the *accidie* of the Desert Fathers which I recognize as part of the way of prayer. But last Sunday it was more than that, and I endeavoured to steer the ship through the stormy waters with a firm hand, neither letting the experience drag me down into the depths of psychic depression nor on the other hand thrashing and kicking against it with my own resources. The middle way of letting things be and calling out in trust and hope in the darkness seems to be the right one in such a case. Powerful, creative prayer may be impossible, but the Psalms are so full of various levels of darkness that I can find solace in the very recognition of my condition there.

A few days have passed since then, and I have learned at least two things. First, the community here is examining its life, with the possibility of quite radical changes in its structure and lifestyle as an enclosed community. I can't write more about it specifically as it is a private matter, though I am privileged to share in prayer in determining the will of God. But I know that there has been much pain and struggle in holding the vision and the courage involved in seeing it through. Some sisters, particularly last Sunday, were in the midst of such experiences. Also a sister of another community who is spending some months at Tymawr testing the solitary life, sometimes passes me a note – and she communicated to me: "I spent the whole of last Sunday morning in tears . . ."

So it was not just me! I suspected that this was the case and it is yet another confirmation of the way in which we are able to enter into darkness, struggle and conflict on behalf of others.

Sometimes the way is much clearer, though it may be difficult. I can be aware that I am called into a participation of a particular kind of darkness for a certain person or event which calls for prayer, fasting and struggle. Mother Mary Clare, during her life, talked to me of such a ministry and the spiritual reserves and psychical balance required to enter into such areas. It can be exceedingly dangerous, however, as I learned to my cost after one particular experience in the Lleyn period.

But last Sunday was one of those occasions in which it was not clear, and I was left in a cloud of unknowing. During this week I am learning what was happening then, and I must allow the passing of the days to minister backwards to me and learn from the experience.

Living completely alone, without speaking to anyone for weeks or months on end is an experience of immense joy.

But it is clear that it can be an experience of pain within joy, too. And depending simply on my own mental resources can be dangerous. All the more reason for me to grow not only in knowledge and maturity, but in simple openness and trust in the love which envelops and indwells me.

There will be times when the feelings and emotional upsurge of joy will be absent. I have always been a "feelings" person, and the emotional content of my Christian (and human) experience has always been high. I have been able to laugh and cry, to dance and sing, to groan and shout in my life of prayer. So when the "sense of God" is not mediated through my feelings and emotions it is a hard journey for me to negotiate.

Over the years I have learned to differentiate between the profound, basic sense of God's presence, and the emotional high that sometimes accompanies it. So there are times when the Lord says: "Ramon, I am taking away those feelings and emotions which you so much enjoy, but you will retain an interior sense of my presence in the darkness and struggle through which I require you to go."

I understand that and accept it. Indeed, it is during such times that real growth takes place, without the emotional gratification which is absent during those periods.

But there is also the experience during which not only the feeling part of religion is denied but also *any* sense of God's loving presence – it is rather a feeling of absence. I am just left without any sign or evidence of his favour and presence. I am still learning to receive such periods, not with resignation or fear, but with the kind of acceptance that takes from God's hand just what he wills to give. I think it was St Catherine of Siena who went through two years of desert aridity in her spiritual life. When she afterwards entered into joy she cried: "Lord, where were you during that awful time?" And he answered: "Catherine, I was not only with you, but sustained you in it all, else you would never have come through." That's it — trusting where I cannot see; believing where I cannot prove.

My favourite prayer during such times is that which is called "St Teresa's bookmark", for she evidently kept it in her prayer-book or Bible, and I would encourage you to learn it before God trusts you with such periods when all feelings are gone and you have to live by naked faith.

Response

* Can you believe that God may intend a creative purpose when he visits you with some form of sorrow or difficulty?

* Can you believe that the Lord wants to remove mere emotional props in your spiritual life so that you may have a firmer foundation based on faith and not simply feelings? Could this be a sign of progress and maturity?

* Will you ask the Lord to enlarge your heart so that you can more closely enter into the sorrows and struggles of your neighbour?

St Teresa's Bookmark

Let nothing disturb you,
Nothing affright you,
All things are passing,
GOD never changes.
Patient endurance
Attains to all things,
Who GOD possesses
In nothing is wanting,
Alone GOD suffices.

ST TERESA OF AVILA

DAY THIRTY-TWO

Enthusing

SCRIPTURE: Isaiah 55:6–13. The joy of creation

Prayer

My Lord God, Joy of Creation:
I thank you for the inflow and upsurge of joy and enthusiasm
in my life.
There are times when your joy overflows in rising and setting
sun, in autumn mists and summer glory, in ebb and flow
of tide and in waxing and waning moon. As in creation so
in redemption, the mingling of melancholy and redeeming
love offer to me the joy that the world can neither give nor
take away.
Grant today that as I enter into joy, the experience may
overflow my life and spread to all those for whom I pray
and whom I love — that the joy of the Lord may be our
strength;
Through Jesus Christ my Lord. Amen.

Reflection

After days of incessant rain my alarm sounded just after 4.00
a.m. today. The morning was crisp, cold and clear. Stars
shone brightly in the night sky as I put my nose out to get
my wellingtons which I'd forgotton to bring in from under
the caravan. I hate them being damp and soggy inside. I was
at my meditation place on my prayer stool before 4.30, for
already I felt that the Lord was preparing for me a day of

positive joy and enthusiasm after the darkness and burden of last Sunday.

The hour was divided this morning. Half of it was a sad but real identification with the incredible and increasing violence between the Serbs and Croats, so soon after their liberation from the common totalitarian enemy. What wounding and rending of the Body of Christ among Orthodox and Roman Catholics there, and what wounding of the body politic too. The rest of the hour was "Be still and know that I am God", and those words came to me as a constant and rhythmic repetition – in the same way as the Jesus Prayer takes over sometimes and carries me into the loving presence of the Lord.

At 5.45 I packed my canvas bag and went up to the convent where I am half-way through painting and decorating the kitchen/scullery/larger area to bring it up to scratch for the inspector of food or hygiene who will come next month.

As I climbed over my enclosure bars I looked through the lightening darkness to where the five joyful horses have been lying for the last few mornings. I couldn't see them but they have a wonderfully large free area of a few acres around me and down to the brook. They are enthusiasm personified, for over the last week they have been incredibly energetic, wildly galloping around and seeming to play games with one another. It is all the more fun when the ground is hard and you can hear their galloping hooves, and their manes and tails are flying in the breeze, and the atmosphere is clouded with their breath – snorting and whinnying with great delight – two of them are colts. How childlike is my appreciation of harmony with the natural world. These creatures reflect my natural enthusiasm, for I am *en-theos* – "in God". He is the source of joy in creation and certainly the source of joy in my soul.

The sheep were lying in groups in the next field as I

climbed over the gate and I told them not to be afraid for it is only me! Then through the next gate where the stocky and overweight horse Brownie is standing, three-and-a-half feet high. She's usually lying down at this time. Her inquisitive partner acknowledges my presence.

It's still dark with enough light to make my way through the last gate. A strip of light is shining from the outside laundry where one of the sisters is probably filling the washing machine (I wonder why she's not at mattins in the chapel). She shines her flashlight on the way to the convent back door and I wait until she is well away and then make my way to the outhouse where I leave my bag and collect the painting materials. I've been scraping, sanding, re-putting and repainting the external window frames around the convent over the last weeks and I'm reluctant to go inside this morning for "the Lord is in the air".

I open the door and the warm air comes to meet me. I must admit that it is a nice feeling to be surrounded by warmth after wearing three sweaters on some days. So I take off my sweaters and put on my painting apron. I've had to cover the strong turquoise paint of the scullery with three coats of vinyl matt brilliant white emulsion. It looks good now and I'm undercoating and glossing the doors and woodwork this morning.

As I work I hear the movement of nuns coming from mattins – some to do their chores, some to prepare convent breakfast and some to their private prayer. After a few minutes all becomes quiet again. No one comes near, though I did surprise one of the sisters this morning on my knees painting the bottom and edges of the open door before I could close it and paint inside again.

As I knelt inside the closed door a note came sliding under it – here are the instructions for the rest of the painting. Nuns have notes down to a fine art – they're far better at it than monks. Convents are full of notes, and some are unconsciously funny. Perhaps I'm being sexist when I say that brothers add naughty additions making notes ridiculous but sisters seem to take them somewhat more seriously.

I don't usually combine jobs but this morning all the logs have disappeared so I'll need to saw up some more for the convent. I finish as much of the gloss as I can for today and then pack up the materials, put on my wellingtons at the outer door, returning to the outhouse.

The cold hits me this time but it is so crisp and clear and the morning sky is beautiful with a reddening glow in the east where the sun is just about to rise over the horizon. My mind goes back to a childhood hymn which I often find myself quietly singing during these early mornings as I see to the hens:

> Every morning the red sun
>   Rises warm and bright;
> But the evening cometh on,
>   And the dark cold night:
> There's a bright land far away
>   Where 'tis never-ending day.

Well, heaven is not far away this morning – it's in my heart. Thoughts of heaven and the life to come are often with me these days. I suppose it is because the number of loved ones who have "crossed the river" increases each year. I think this morning of my father and mother whom I miss greatly and two dear friends of my age who met sudden death by accident over the last two years. Hymns on heaven are not popular these days but I find myself playing through the "heaven" sections in my catholic and evangelical hymn books, as a way of meditating. I suppose the veil between this world and the next is thinner when one lives in solitude – certainly it is for me.

I collect my pail of chicken feed, fill another pail with water and go down to the first chicken run. They hear me coming and begin clucking and edging toward the flap-door as I clang the pails. The first henhouse contains the older chickens and they are more circumspect in emerging through the flap, except for the brown-and-white pair of bantams who are always clucking and running before anyone else. I notice that the first signs of winter ice are forming in the water containers.

In the second run I fill the troughs with feed before I open the big door, for they flap and fly and run out immediately with great gusto as if they've never seen chicken feed before. I change the water, clean the houses, piling the muck on the heap outside.

Then I get the wheelbarrow, saw, axe, hammer and wedge and go to the woodpile. I only need one of my sweaters for this is a warm job and as I begin sawing the sun breaks through the surrounding clouds and fills the world with glory.

Joy and tears are so close in my experience these days and immense gratitude wells up to the Lord for my feeling of well-being in manual work today. I spend forty minutes or so sawing and chopping and fill a box with logs, then take the tools back to the toolshed. I fill my water container, pack my canvas bag and pick up a postcard which has been left in my box in the tractor shed.

The card has been redirected from Glasshampton and is from Bill, a Baptist minister friend who is leading a group in the Holy Land – another glimpse of glory in a day which I feel is full of promise.

It says: "Dear Ramon, how you would love this land – I have prayed for you in many holy places and thought of you as we saw hermitages in the Judean hills. *Shalom* from Israel. PS I am just watching sun-up on the Mount of Olives! Bill."

Bill loves the Holy Land and we sometimes swap a bit of the Hebrew we've kept up from theological college. A card like this brings back all the fellowship I've shared with him and I pray for him, his family and ministry at Teddington. We've prayed for one another faithfully since we were fifteen years of age – one of those friendships which not only survives different denominational allegiances but which grows and matures in love and in the sharing of sorrows.

I chuckle to myself as I remember the evangelism we used to do together, going "pubbing" on Saturday nights with a pile of tracts and gospels, getting embroiled in difficult situations with groups of drunks and spending hours around the seamier parts of Swansea – getting "roughed up" sometimes. From pub-evangelist to hermit – well, the jump is not so great I think. Certainly St Francis of Assisi would not find any contradiction there.

By this time I climb over the bars back into my orchard, make some coffee, put on my breakfast porridge to cook slowly and prepare for morning prayer. Saying morning prayer five-and-a-half hours after getting up sounds a bit daft but the wonderful thing about the hermit life is that it is *idio-rhythmic* – which could be translated "doing your own thing", but means that the timetable is sometimes turned on its head by the Lord.

In the middle of manual work he can call me into prayer and there is no one and nothing which has prior claim – save sometimes my own stupidity and sin. I'm looking forward to morning prayer today for I shall play and sing one of my favourite of Charles Wesley's hymns: "Jesus the Name high over all" to the great tune Lydia – one of my great *en-theos* hymns. It's worth learning by heart. I end today's reflection with two of the stanzas.

Response

* Note down a few things that have enthused you in your life.

215

* Have you ever felt enthused by the person of Jesus in the gospels, and if so, has that experience increased or diminished?

* Enthusiasm does not have to be emotional. Write down ways in which you think a Christian may channel his/her enthusiasm.

Jesus! the Name high over all,
    In hell, or earth, or sky;
Angels and men before it fall,
    And devils fear and fly . . .

O that the world might taste and see
    The riches of His grace;
The arms of love that compass me
    Would all mankind embrace.

CHARLES WESLEY

Failing

SCRIPTURE: 1 Kings 19:1–21. Elijah – the failure of a vocation?

Prayer

O God of faithfulness and patience, you grant your people a vision of holiness and love, and call us to fulfil that vision in our earthly lives. When a sense of failure overwhelms us, the powers of darkness engulf us and the baseness of our motives threatens us – then in faithfulness hold us close to your heart and in patience deal with us tenderly. Thus renewed in vision and cleansed in motive our feet shall once again be set upon the path of your will;
Through Jesus Christ our Lord. Amen.

Reflection

No prophet had a greater sense of vocation than Elijah. Consumed with burning zeal and with a divine commission he waited upon God, confronted Ahab, challenged the prophets of Baal on Mount Carmel, striding through the Old Testament like a spiritual giant. But in our reading, fleeing from Queen Jezebel, he is trembling with fear and exhaustion, heavy with depression and convinced of the failure of his vocation:

He went a day's journey into the desert. He came to a broom tree, sat down under it and prayed that he might die. "I have had enough, Lord," he said. "Take my life; I am no better than my ancestors."

I have never felt this radical sense of utter despondency. Neither had I previously experienced the apprehension of failure that is written over this incident. But it did begin to happen to me during the second year of this present extended solitude.

Don't get me wrong. It is not a fear for my salvation. After all, we are not saved by spiritual athletic prowess or charismatic showmanship but by the grace of God. The basis of my salvation is the love and mercy revealed in Jesus Christ. I am talking about a failure of vocation.

There were times when Elijah's vision was filled with the glory of God's flaming holiness, when he was drawn irresistibly by God's Spirit and his eyes were blinded to lesser things. I also have been constrained to use that kind of language to express something of the wonder of the divine Love which has always moved and drawn me to itself.

Holiness and union with God is the wider call to every Christian, but there is also a personal vocation to which we must respond. Increasingly, over the last decade or more, I have felt drawn into a deeper life of prayer and solitude. My longing for such solitude was only increased by the experimental weeks and months spent alone with God and seemed to confirm the rightness of the path I was following with the support of my community.

Often I have shed tears of love and longing for a closer walk with God and have not doubted the rightness of this vocation – whether it led to longer or shorter times of solitude. But when the crunch came, and I began an open-ended period of the hermit life in 1990, it followed my predicted path for the first year. But during the second year I was visited by times of apprehension and fear of failure.

It was not the vocation that I doubted, but my ability to

218

persevere, to maintain the vision, to trust myself to God wholly in the darkness and unknowing that is necessarily a part of this way.

More than ever I believed in the validity of the vocation of the hermit life in the Church of God and I could not cease to believe that I had been caught up in that tradition which is rooted in the prophetic vocation of the Old Testament.

There were glimpses of darkness on ahead even during the first year, but into the second year I began to identify with the prophets not only in their call and burning desire for God but, for the first time at such depth, with the emptiness and sense of failure that some of them experienced.

Yet it was not as noble as that. If I could have said, "Oh yes, this is the time-worn, well-trodden path that prophets and saints have walked – I must gird up my loins to battle with doubt and darkness," then that would have been positive. But there was, for the first time in my long Christian experience, the possibility of failure. And I remembered Donald Crowhurst.

It was in the early 1970s that I came across the story of a failure which deeply impressed itself upon my mind with its great pathos and tragedy in a book called *The Strange Voyage of Donald Crowhurst*. Lately I found a retelling of it in Chris Bonington's *Quest for Adventure*.

In the chapter "The Golden Globe" he relates the story of the *Sunday Times* contest for the first "non-stop around the world single-handed boat race" beginning in 1968 with nine contestants. It's a wonderfully thrilling adventure, well illustrated, revealing the vision, courage and skill of the men who participated. Only one finished the voyage. Seven others nobly did not – but one failed in the most profound and fearful way.

Donald Crowhurst was thirty-five years old at the time. In the RAF he had gained a reputation as a superficial adventurer, racing around in souped-up cars, smashing a

Lagonda, until he was asked to leave the service. He went into the army but lost his licence for a variety of driving offences and was obliged to resign his commission. His firm, Electron Utilisation in Bridgwater, was nearly bankrupt, and the challenge of the Golden Globe contest was attractive. It would solve his financial problems, enable him to make a grand gesture, especially in outsailing Francis Chichester whom he disliked, and make people sit up and take notice. So he approached the Cutty Sark Trust asking if he might charter *Gipsy Moth IV*, but was turned down.

The 31st October was the last day for any contestant to set off, so from May to October he had his trimaran (a boat with three connected hulls) built. Harassed by his energetic press agent he chased around the country for extra sponsorship, ignoring the essential but minor details of construction and equipping the boat *Teignmouth Electron*.

As the time drew near he became engulfed by anxieties and doubts but maintained an up-front bravado. He and his wife Clare spent the night of 30th October at a Teignmouth hotel, and Bonington writes:

> He admitted to Clare that the boat was just not up to the voyage and asked whether she would go out of her mind with worry. With hindsight she realized that he was asking her to stop him going, but she did not see it at the time and did her best to reassure him. He cried through the rest of the night.

The story is intriguing but full of pathos. The route from the south coast of Britain went down into the South Atlantic, rounding South Africa's Cape of Good Hope in the Southern Ocean, through the Roaring Forties, into the Pacific past Australia and New Zealand, around Cape Horn and back up into the South Atlantic, North Atlantic and home.

Crowhurst's fictional and forged route followed this pattern, but his actual route never took him out of the

Atlantic Ocean. On 19th January he radioed that he was a hundred miles south-east of Gough Island to the west of the Cape of Good Hope, and he cut off radio communication.

He dallied in the South Atlantic until April when he linked up his radio again, claiming that he was approaching Cape Horn when he was actually off the coast of Argentina.

He was now involved in a massive fraud, circling the wastes of the South Atlantic all those months, avoiding shipping lanes, forging a log and sustaining an immense lie.

Falsifying the circumnavigation involved deceit at other levels too, and his journal and tape recordings indicated mental disorientation with introspective poems and reflections.

The crunch came when the competitor he hoped would stay ahead of him struck tragedy and sank in the Azores. This was Nigel Tetley in the *Victress*, whose coming second after Robin Knox-Johnston's victory would have ensured that Crowhurst's logs and story would not come under close scrutiny. It was at this point that he realized that he could not bring together his factual and fictional routes and stories. His last log entry on 1st July, still annotated with the time, was both a confession and a declaration of suicide:

> 11.15.00 It is the end of
> my game; the truth
> has been revealed and it will
> be done as my family requires me
> to do it

> 11.17.00 It is the time for your
> move to begin
> I have not need to prolong
> the game
> It has been a good game that
> must be ended at the . . .

> I will play this game when
> I will chose I will resign the
> game 11.20.40 there is
> no reason for harmful

These were the last words he wrote. The *Teignmouth Electron* was spotted on 10th July by the Royal Mail Vessel *Picardy*. Like the *Marie Celeste* she was ghosting along under her mizzen sail. There was no one aboard, the cabin was cluttered with tools and electronic gear, the dishes and pans dirty in the sink, and the logs with their damning witness on the chart table.

In his summing-up of the nine contestants Bonington speaks of the positive formative influence the experience had upon them, but:

> Crowhurst, on the other hand, was engulfed by the experience. Enamoured of a venture that was beyond him, he found himself on an escalator built by the media and other people's expectations from which he could not escape. He had set out in a boat that was ill-prepared and, in all probability, would have foundered in the Southern Ocean, but while Ridgway and Fougeron, who had found themselves in similar circumstances, had retired with honour, Crowhurst could not bring himself to admit that his dreams of glory were over. Having allowed fantasy to lead him into fraud, when it became inevitable that his deception would be discovered, his mind escaped from reality and he committed suicide.

There is honourable and dishonourable failure. Poor Crowhurst began with some vision and skill, though his motives were suspect from the first, as Francis Chichester realized. The sadness I feel in relating this story is that in periods of darkness and doubt – such as Elijah's – I examine my own apprehensions and ask questions about the purity of my motives and the level of my own hypocrisy. I ask if my own profound desire to follow the solitary path is not reflected in the attitude of a man like Donald Crowhurst.

I realize at such times how important are the warnings in the tradition about the spiritual and psychological maturity of the novice, and the purity of heart which is involved in such a journey. I can see now, as never before, how it is possible for a man or woman to become entangled in a solitary path which leads, not to fulfilment of a vocation to love for God and service in the world, but to bondage to dark powers which lure him or her on to spiritual suicide.

There have been times during this last period when I have wanted to withdraw, not only from this present solitude, but from the religious life itself, full of fears of my own inability to answer the vision and vocation, together with the awareness of my own hypocrisy in pretending to a depth of prayer in God that eludes me.

But that is not the whole story. When I come to the place of tears and confession before God and before my spiritual director, I realize again that this is part of the way which is new to me because I am not used to confessions of failure and hypocrisy in this sense. I return to Scripture, to the Desert Father tradition, and as often before, find some relevant and humorous words from Thomas Merton, which speak to my condition. They occur in a letter he wrote to Fr Callistus Peterson OCSO in answer to questions about the evolution of the Cistercian life, and I conclude this chapter with them.

Response

Comment on the following questions in your journal:

* Do you recognize that self-doubt and awareness of failure is part of the way of discipleship?

* Are you willing to face your own commitment and vocation honestly before God, listening to what God is saying?

* Are you willing to share areas of doubt and uncertainty, together with your hopes and vision for the future, with a soul friend/spiritual director so that things may be seen objectively and in clearer perspective?

I see clearer than ever that I am not a monk, still less a Cistercian monk, and that I have no business making statements that directly affect the conduct of the Cistercian life (except to try to help my novices live without going nuts . . .). With this unpleasant clarity I expect to try to live for a few more years, hoping that I will not go nuts myself. This, I think, is about the best that I can hope for. It sums up the total of my expectations for the immediate future. If on top of this the Lord sees fit in His mercy to admit me to a non-monastic corner of heaven, among the beatniks and pacifists and other maniacs, I will be exceedingly grateful. Doubtless there will be a few pseudo-hermits among them and we will all sit around and look at each other and wonder how we made it. Up above will be the monks, with a clearer view of their own status and a more profound capacity to appreciate the meaning of status and a more profound capacity to appreciate the meaning of status and the value of having one.

THOMAS MERTON

DAY THIRTY-FOUR

Aspiring

SCRIPTURE: Philippians 3:10–21. Pressing on towards the goal

Prayer

Father of mercy and compassion:
You call all humankind to the healing of body, mind and
spirit, and give to each one a specific task and vocation
in love;
Give me the faith to respond to your salvation,
the wisdom to discern my particular vocation,
the strength and vision to live it out joyfully
and at last, with all your people, to receive its consum-
mation in glory;
Through Jesus Christ my Lord. Amen.

Reflection

Beset by doubt yet filled with hope. Here apprehension and aspiration mingle together. No voyager on sea, land or air embarks on a new journey without maps or guides. There are exceptions like Abraham who was called by God to go out not knowing where he was bound for, or the Celtic monks who set out on the wide sea throwing away their oars so that they would be cast wholly upon God. But when there are maps and guides to help you then it would be stupid not to consult them beforehand and throughout. But it is, nevertheless, one thing to see a terrain marked on a map and quite another to walk, ride, sail or fly into the area the map depicts.

I knew there was *accidie*, tribulation, dark night of the soul and a confrontation with psychic and dark powers – the maps and spiritual guides told me so – but to be exposed to blackness, depression and terror was not what I imagined it would be.

Also I knew there would be a cloud of unknowing, a walking by faith when all sense of God's loving presence would be withdrawn, but I didn't reckon on the nakedness of its feeling reality or that there would be such deep probing and doubt about my own motives. Yet at the same time that the apostle Paul was aware of the possibility of his own disqualification from the race (1 Corinthians 9:27) he was also expending all the energies of body and spirit in an aspiring yearning to enter into the deepest knowledge of God possible this side of heaven:

> I want to know Christ and the power of his resurrection and the fellowship of sharing in his sufferings, becoming like him in his death, and so, somehow, to attain to the resurrection from the dead. Not that I have already obtained all this, or have already been made perfect, but I press on to take hold of that for which Christ Jesus took hold of me . . . I do not consider myself yet to have taken hold of it. But one thing I do: Forgetting what is behind and straining towards what is ahead, I press on towards the goal to win the prize for which God has called me heavenwards in Christ Jesus. (Philippians 3:10–14)

The sad story of Donald Crowhurst which I've just related made me realize that there is a path to hell from the very gate of heaven and that God's grace must not be presumed upon. There must be a *basic* motivation towards God even if motives are sometimes mixed and often unclear. Crowhurst reminds me that deceit and hypocrisy are always possible, perhaps even more dangerously in the utterly sincere religious person – for religious zeal often leads to fanaticism – and it is clear where that leads in the darker history of the Church.

But if the deterioration of Crowhurst makes me tremble with doubt and apprehension, my attention fixes upon another of the Golden Globe contestants. His name is Bernard Moitessier and he represents the person who lives in an amazing detachment from money, reputation, competition and publicity.

He was born in Saigon, spent his early years in the Far East in cargo-carrying junks and then in boats built by himself, sailing around the Pacific and Indian oceans. He already held the long-distance record for small boats, having sailed from Tahiti to Portugal – 14,212 miles.

By the beginning of the Golden Globe contest he was a lean, ascetic-looking man of forty-three years, a romantic adventurer who loved the sea with an intense, almost mystical passion. It was the voyage of 30,000 miles, alone in the oceans with the wind and wild seas that was the attraction, not the record, the money or the reputation. He hated the publicity of attracting funds and planned to sail *Joshua*, the boat he had built himself.

There were two prizes in the contest – the Golden Globe trophy for the first one to complete the circumnavigation, and £5,000 for the fastest time. Robin Knox-Johnston made it for the trophy, but it became clear that Moitessier was going to make it for the cash prize, though he was not interested in money or competition. Before setting off he said: "The people who are thinking about money and of being the fastest round the world will not win. It is the people who care about their skins. I shall bring back my skin, apart from a few bumps on the head."

The effect of battling with the hazards of ocean, storms and especially solitude are spelled out in Bonington's account. He quotes John Ridgway, caught in a wild squall in his *English Rose IV*:

> A bitter struggle began on the foredeck as I fought to recover both sails; the wind shrieked with glee. In the end it was down and I crept below and burst into tears; for some reason I could not shake off the emotional strain of the loneliness. I noted that I cried at some point on each of the twenty-seven consecutive days.

Moitessier, on the other hand, was not only weathering the storms but glorying in the solitude:

> The days go by, never monotonous. Even when they appear exactly alike they are never quite the same. That is what gives life at sea its special dimension, made up of contemplation and very simple contrasts. Sea, wind, calms, sun, clouds, porpoises. Peace and the joy of being alive in harmony.

When everyone believed that Moitessier was somewhere in the mid-Atlantic approaching the Equator and nearing the final run for home, he was suddenly sighted off the Cape of Good Hope. He sailed into the outer reaches of the harbour and catapulted a message for the *Sunday Times* on to the bridge of an anchored tanker. It read: "The Horn was rounded February 5, and today is March 18. I am continuing non-stop towards the Pacific Islands because I am happy at sea and perhaps also to save my soul."

People could hardly believe it. How could he, with success and glory in his grasp, reject it in this way? The *Sunday Times* tried to get a message from his wife through to him, asking him to return to Plymouth and telling him that the whole of France was waiting for his victory and return. But he never received the message and although he had originally intended to return to Plymouth he was afraid that he would be drawn into what he felt was the falsity of the situation, into a society that he considered was destroying itself with materialism, pollution and violence.

So he sailed round the Cape of Good Hope for the second time into the wild winds and seas of the southern winter. This was a much rougher voyage than the first time. He was knocked down four times as he sailed past Australia, New Zealand and then into the South Pacific towards Tahiti, which he reached on 21st June 1969, having sailed one-and-a-half times around the world single-handed. There, he told journalists that he had never intended to race:

> Talking of records is stupid. An insult to the sea. The thought of a competition is grotesque. You have to understand that when one is months and months alone, one evolves; some people say, go nuts. I went crazy in my own fashion. For four months all I saw were the stars. I didn't hear an unnatural sound. A purity grows out of that kind of solitude. I said to myself, "What the hell am I going to do in Europe?" I told myself I'd be crazy to go on to France.

The voyage was sufficient in itself. He rejected the competition, the prize and the fame. There had been talk of him receiving the Legion of Honour in France. But it was not his rejection that was important or primary but the affirmation of his own lifestyle and independence. His aspiration involved the rejection of society's values, but it was an aspiration towards solitude and the love of open sea and sky.

It is not difficult for me to see my own aspiration and pilgrimage in parallel with many of those in Bonington's collection. The whole idea of quest, pilgrimage, adventure, risks, goals, navigational, intuitive and psychological skills, battles and confrontations are involved continually. Also the whole area of human relationships, self-discovery and the challenge of solitude are at the heart of such a journey.

Crowhurst represents the ultimate danger and failure, and Moitessier represents the purified aspiration which never rests in what has been accomplished but reaches out to salvation in its widest sense.

My journey is a spiritual one, and is the journey of all men and women. God is its source, continuity and end. To each of us he gives a particular, a special vocation, within the wider call to salvation. After laying before God my own failure, hypocrisy, mixture of motives and fearful anxieties, the quest sounds again in my inward heart:

Therefore, since we are surrounded by such a great cloud of witnesses, let us throw off everything that hinders and the sin that so easily entangles, and let us run with perseverance the race marked out for us. Let us fix our eyes on Jesus, the author and perfecter of our faith, who for the joy set before him endured the cross, scorning its shame, and sat down at the right hand of the throne of God. (Hebrews 12:1–2)

Response

* Do you identify with either Crowhurst or Moitessier in this and the previous chapters?

* Write down points of identification with each/either.

* Can you affirm, in spite of your failures, hypocrisy and double-dealing, the mercy and compassion of a God who understands and continues to call you ever deeper into the mystery of his love?

Thoughts of packing it in came into my mind for the first time today, brought on I think by too much of my own company. It would be so easy to put into port and say that the boat was not strong enough for the voyage or unsuitable. What was really upsetting me was the psychological effect – of possibly twelve months – this might have. Would I be the same person on return? This aspect I knew worried Eve too. I nearly put through a radio call to talk over the question in guarded terms. Then I realized that though she would straightaway accept the reason and agree to my stopping, say at Cape Town, we would feel that we had let ourselves down both in our own eyes and those of our friends, backers and well-wishers. It was only a touch of the blues due to the yacht's slow progress.

NIGEL TETLEY, *contestant
in the Golden Globe contest*

DAY THIRTY-FIVE

Loving

SCRIPTURE: romans 8:31–39. The height and depth of love

Prayer

Heavenly Father: As Creator you loved us before we were born, as Sustainer you love us at every moment of our lives and as Redeemer you will love us through the ages of eternity. Help us to understand that love which is unconditional and eternal and may our lives reflect its glory and shine with its beauty, lighting up the darkest places of our world;
Through Jesus Christ our Lord. Amen.

Reflection

I was stunned some time ago on hearing one of our friars tell a true story in a sermon. It concerned a boy who consented to give blood for his older sister who had leukaemia because they were of the same blood-group. As he lay there when the blood was being taken he asked the nurse: "How long will it be before I die?" He actually thought it would cost him his life, yet he had simply said "yes".

Stories like this make me glad again that I am a human being, though they also make me wonder if I presume when I claim to know about love. But it's no use denying it, I imbibed love with my mother's milk and have been sustained by it in my pilgrimage through the years. This is why I have been able to weather experiences of loneliness and loss and have been able to love others as well as to properly esteem my own worth.

It is sad to find a man who cannot love others because he has been rejected from childhood or a woman who cannot love God because of the oppression and abuse directed towards her from her own father and mother.

I do not say that a person *cannot* love because of such deficiencies in childhood or in him/herself, for love can always find a way. But it is certainly much more difficult to overcome such obstacles in the experience of loving.

There are so many personal illustrations of love in my own life, but two lie deep within my heart which I can share now that my parents have died but which were too precious to bring out while they were still alive.

The first goes back many years but it is indelibly impressed upon my heart. I obtained a part-scholarship to a commercial school when I was thirteen but the fees were still difficult for my parents. So I took a paper-boy job on weekdays and a butcher-boy job in Swansea market on Saturdays (I sometimes think my vegetarianism began there!). Yet at the beginning of one term it was impossible to get the school fees together.

My mother did not tell my father or myself but did something which amazed me when I discovered it, and has not ceased to amaze me down the years since. She actually pawned her wedding ring.

No one would have been any the wiser if my father had not found the pawn-ticket when rummaging upstairs for something else, but I remember him coming down the stairs two at a time and demanding: "Edna, what is this?"

And it all came out. Eventually my fees that term were paid by Trevor, one of the deacons at my home church, but I shall never forget or undervalue that act of love which causes me to tremble at the telling of it now.

The second story happened just four months before my father's death in 1988. He had become frail and blind, and after my mother had cared for him at home for two years or so, he was admitted to hospital and then transferred to a local nursing home.

My mother had ophthalmic surgery by that time and could no longer manage him at home and I visited a few days together every month from Glasshampton, for my father could only relate to the immediate family by then. I knew he was lonely and longed to be back in his own bed at home. You can imagine how I felt, looking after some of the old and sick friars at Glasshampton when my own father was needing so much care.

It was the kind of dilemma which many people have with their elderly and frail parents. He would not have gone to my sister's family for with four children it would have been too noisy for him. So I decided I must do something.

One sunny September day, wanting to give him the opportunity, I took him in a wheel-chair to St James' park. After a little talking with periods of silence – that was the way it often was – I said to him: "Dad, I want to ask you something." He inclined his head a little towards me for he could not see. "You don't want to stay in the nursing home do you? You'd prefer to be at home?" He murmured his agreement not wanting to commit himself to anything.

"Well, you know that mam can't manage you on her own now, but what if I get six months or more leave from the Society so that I can look after you at home?"

He asked me some questions about my mother and we talked it over for a minute or two and then he said: "Son, I think I'd better stay where I am for the present."

Then I said: "You know why I ask, don't you? Because I love you." And he began to weep quietly, and so did I. Then he replied: "And I love you too." Then he started to sing:

> There may be grey skies,
> I don't mind those grey skies,
> You make them blue, sonny-boy.

and there we were — dad in his wheelchair and me on the
park bench in a clerical collar, both singing:

> Friends may forsake me,
> Let them all forsake me,
> For I have you, sonny-boy . . .

Too sentimental for words — but a moment which lies deep
in my heart, in which we confessed and affirmed love for
each other as never before. Though there were visits and talks
and singing during the following few months, that is the last
distinct and indelible memory which I covet of my father.

My sister and I have a cassette which contains both our
parents talking and singing together, including another
sentimental song: "You were meant for me . . ." but we are
afraid to play it, for we should both cry together. How much
we miss them!

Because of their love I was able to recognize the love of
God in Jesus when I was twelve years of age and began to
love him then. The mingling in my life of loves human and
divine have enabled me to be open to the world of nature
and to all things good and true and life-giving, for I have
always seen them as manifestations of love.

That is not to say that I have not caused people hurt and
grief and harm in my life, but I have always been brought
to sorrow because of it. My sensitivity to love and gentleness
has made me vulnerable in a violent world, but my desire
to protect the weak has made me strong.

Following a non-violent path pays its own dividends, for
when I made a singular stand at seventeen years of age
against military conscription I left my office job for the world
of hospital and caring. This led on to theological college

and university and then caring for people in a parish and students in a university chaplaincy.

Community life among the Franciscans with its demands made use of my various communicative and counselling abilities, with an emphasis upon the life of prayer which has brought me into the solitude I longed for. And here I reflect upon the thread of love which has been interwoven into the whole pattern of my life, being the strongest thread and brightest colour in the whole cloth.

If you have read these words with some fellow-feeling, you will realize that openness to love is openness to life. St John of the Cross said that where there is no love you should pour love in, and then you would draw love out. And he wrote these lovely words: "When the evening of this life comes we shall be judged by love."

This is not contradicted by the violence of an ungodly world, for if you respond to violence with love then love is victorious. The Christian is not so naive as to believe that the world will often respond to love with love. Jesus is the pattern, and if the world hated and crucified him it will hate and crucify the believer also. Therefore our reading today from the letter to the Romans contains words which are among the most beautiful in Scripture, and cause me to catch my breath with the sheer wonder of their revelation. There is nothing in heaven, earth or hell that can separate us from the love of Christ.

So at the end of this world's day it will be clear that the only way to live and die is the way of love. The One who prayed, "Father, forgive them, for they know not what they do . . ." will bring us all into the fullness of his Father's answer to that prayer.

Response

∗ Look back to your childhood. Write down any memories

of sadness, rejection or lack of sympathy. Consider them prayerfully and write down words of forgiveness and understanding.

* Then write down any memories of love, security, acceptance and warmth. Put down words of gratitude for such experiences.

* Can you see that love is the cord which binds all compassionate life together and manifests the love of God who will draw all those who love to himself at last?

To Be Capable of Love

To be capable of love is a very precious, a very human potentiality. If you have found your own depths moved in love, then be thankful and let your joy spill over the boundaries of your own life. It begins with a sheer gift of grace, a warm flow of life and energy that enables you to love your deepest self in response to the love which embraces you on every side. Parental love can be received and reciprocated, and from such a vantage point of security and warmth you will be able to demonstrate love for the inanimate created order, for the animal creation, for friends, neighbours and strangers. And then to fall in love . . . to give yourself to another and to be received in love. All this is a training ground for the love of God to flow and overflow, so that you will be able to love the poor, the weak, the oppressed and the ugly . . . to love those who cannot or will not return your love . . . and to love those who hate and persecute you.

And where is the origin, the inspiration and source of such love? It is in God.

Remembering

SCRIPTURE: Luke 23:32–43. "Jesus, remember me."

Prayer

We remember the days gone by, dear Lord, and we bless you. You have surrounded us by your protecting love and forgiven and delivered us from all our sins and stupidities; Keep us faithful to you as you have been faithful to us, and enable us to trust you more for all our future days; Through Jesus Christ our Lord. Amen.

Reflection

I have a good memory. Of things past, I mean. Like throwing a bottle of milk over the stairs for my father to catch when I was two years old (he missed it!), and shortly afterwards getting my head stuck between the uprights of the bannisters so that I had to be sawn out.

I recall a memorable tenth year when I was at the "roundtop" school. If you look up to your right as you enter Swansea past the docks you can see the red circular building perched three miles above the city. I still take a solitary walk up there when I visit, for I love to sit on the sloping grass bank in front of the school and survey the five-mile coastline from Swansea to Mumbles pier with the city laid out before me. It stirs up memories.

Our much-loved teacher was Noel Davies. Paddy Birmingham and I shared the same tenth birthday – he gave us tenpence each. It was he who said: "Remember, boys, he who takes the sword shall perish with the sword." I've never forgotten it.

Then there was that wonderful day when he gave me a copy of *Child Education* with its centrefold colour plate. I don't think he realized the significance of that magic moment for me. *Child Education* contained the world of words, poetry, pictures, stories, puzzles, projects which wrapped up that mysterious dimension of communication represented by Noel. By such a gift he shared with me the spheres of truth and beauty and hinted that there was room there for me.

In that tenth year, too, because I lived a street below the usual catchment area, the time came when we all had to transfer schools – everybody else up to Townhill and me down to Waun Wen. I remember crying with loss and sadness – the feeling remains with me today. Memories of regret never really lose their melancholy, as the apostle Peter proved, looking back on that sad denial of his Lord. The text is a poignant one:

> The Lord turned and looked straight at Peter. Then Peter remembered the word the Lord had spoken to him: "Before the cock crows today, you will disown me three times." And he went outside and wept bitterly. (Luke 22:61f.)

Sad memories can often be redeemed, but not always. I remember first being strangely moved as a boy reading in my cherished *Palgrave's Golden Treasury* the poem by Thomas Hood:

> I remember, I remember
>   The house where I was born
> The little window where the sun
>   Came peeping in at morn;

He never came a wink too soon
  Nor brought too long a day;
But now, I often wish the night
  Had borne my breath away! . . .

I remember, I remember
  The fir trees dark and high;
I used to think their slender tops
  Were close against the sky:
It was a childish ignorance,
  But now 'tis little joy
To know I'm farther off from Heaven
  than when I was a boy.

These two stanzas especially communicated their sadness and I lingered over them wondering what could have happened to steal his joy away.

I spend a great deal of time remembering here in my hermitage, for "remember me" has been on my lips and on the lips of those who have asked me to pray for them. Remembering is praying in my prayers of intercession, and also as I recall the sadness and joy of my life as it passes before me. Sad and bitter memories can be redeemed as they are brought out into the open and held before the healing love of God. Memories of cruelty and rejection can be transformed by prayers of confession and forgiveness even if some of the people concerned have died. The bitter retort or angry disagreement which was not resolved before the death of a former friend or relative can be lifted up to the love of God. The celebration of a requiem eucharist can be the place of reconciliation and the healing of memories. I often hold warm, loving, compassionate, joyful memories before the Lord in gratitude, praise and song. I remind the Lord of his faithfulness in days gone by (for my sake, not his!) and affirm his love for the present and future, saying, "Do it again, Lord!"

The Psalms are full of this kind of praying as the Psalmist cries out, thirsty for the living God in remembrance of past days of blessing (42:4) and through the watches of the night affirming that they will return (63:7). In the midst of exile, persecution and desertion psalms of remembrance rise from hearts that are faint and desolate (137:1), and even in direct confrontation with enemies who threaten to crush his life to the ground, the psalmist remembers the God who cares and delivers from fear and evil (143:5).

"Remember me" is an arrow prayer which arises from a longing heart. Hannah prays this prayer as she longs for a child (1 Samuel 1:11); Joseph prays it incarcerated unjustly in prison (Genesis 40:14); Samson prays it in his blindness and weakness after he has been taunted as a fool (Judges 16:28). Jeremiah prays it as his enemies close in to destroy him (Jeremiah 15:15); Hezekiah prays it after sentence of death, crying for reprieve (2 Kings 20:3).

All these prayers are heard and answered. Perhaps the penitent thief who was crucified with Jesus had heard these stories from his childhood, for when the impenitent thief taunted Jesus he rebuked him, and turning in his dying agony to the crucified Saviour he prayed the same prayer which had sounded down through Jewish history and was answered by the God who receives the penitent and forgives: "Jesus, remember me when you come into your kingdom." Jesus answered him, "I tell you the truth, today you will be with me in paradise."

Memory is so alive for me that I often take a memory walk as a way of praying. I go walking in a quiet place and select a memory from my rich tapestry of experience and talk it through with the Lord. It may be a precious memory of my parents or loved ones in which great joy and some rich humour is uppermost. Or it may be a sad memory of failure, broken relationships, a misunderstanding or bitter words spoken in a reactionary moment and ever since regretted.

241

Travelling through the memory I speak in the present to those who inhabit the memory with me — affirming love, confessing sorrow or righting moments, words and experiences which may have gone awry. And because this is done in the presence of the Lord he pours his blessing and healing into the memories and puts right things beyond my power to change.

Recently reading Gerard Hughes' *Walking to Jerusalem* I found that he does something similar. His long walking pilgrimage gave him much time for reflection, and in recalling special places like the Isle of Iona, he talks about how thin the veil is that separates the saints from the praying soul. I quote the passage at the end of this chapter to indicate that what I am saying is not a novel experience but one in which memory and imagination can combine in an all-embracing prayer which breaks down the barriers of time and space, making us aware not only of the communion of saints but of the near presence of our dear Lord.

Response

* Spend some time in reflecting upon years gone by and write down one of your saddest memories.

* Do the same in writing down one of your happiest memories.

* Talk through both these memories with the Lord, asking him to heal and redeem the sadness, giving thanks and praise for the gladness.

The Veil is Thin Here

On the road to Jerusalem I caught many glimpses of the thin veil. As I walked the roads I often thought of those Celtic monks, who wandered through Europe, wondering at the glory of God's creation, preaching the Gospel and founding monasteries. At first they were imaginary figures from the distant past, but they are in God, who is eternal, that is, always in the now, in the God who keeps my legs going along these roads, so those Celtic saints are as near to me as the living, in fact nearer. Why shouldn't St Patrick cheer me up on the road, just as the waitress cheered me by lighting the candle on the table? Following this line of thought, I found myself talking with these figures from the past and with my own dead relatives and friends, especially with my sister Marie, who had died forty years earlier. These conversations became very natural and they could be very helpful in decision making. I realise, even as I write, that this will sound as odd to some readers as it would have seemed to me before I tried it.

GERARD HUGHES

Theologizing

SCRIPTURE: John 20:24–29. From experience to theology

Prayer

You who are the light of the minds that know you, the life of the souls that love you and the strength of the wills that serve you: Help us so to know you that we may truly love you, so to love you that we may fully serve you, whom to serve is perfect freedom. Amen.

Reflection

"Thomas the doubter became Thomas the shouter?" I've remembered that sentence from a sermon I heard on today's reading when I was a boy. The reason I've remembered it is because it plucked a chord of experience in my young heart.

The scene is set in a dramatic context in the twentieth chapter of John's Gospel. We are presented with powerful pictures proclaiming the risen Christ. First of all in the early morning, when Mary Magdalene, Peter and John come to the garden they are faced with an empty tomb (vv. 1–10).

Then as Mary is left alone, weeping, the risen Christ comes to her with tenderness and calm assurance (11–18). There follows an appearance of Jesus to the trembling disciples in the locked upper room, imparting peace and showing them his wounded but risen body (19–23). Then

244

comes the dramatic scene of our reading.

Thomas had been absent when Jesus appeared but when he returned he found a charged atmosphere, a bewildered but exultant group of disciples and a witness that Jesus had appeared to them in the body in which he had been crucified.

Thomas's cautious and phlegmatic reaction to that incredible tale revealed his unbelief: "Unless I see the nail marks in his hands and put my finger where the nails were, and put my hand into his side, I will not believe it." Then came the mind-blowing experience.

A week had passed and Thomas was with the disciples, having no doubt been involved in frustrating arguments which made his grief in bereavement even harder to bear. The doors were still locked and the room secure, but suddenly without warning, and radiating with life and power, Jesus stood before them with words of peace.

He looked at Thomas and said: "Thomas, put your finger here; see my hands. Reach out your hand and put it into my side. Stop doubting and believe."

Thomas gazed upon those wounds of glory, felt joy flooding his being and fell down before Jesus confessing his faith: "My Lord and my God." In that moment experience became theology and that form of words which gave voice to the reality of the resurrection is at the same time a confession of the divinity of Christ.

The two powerful words which make up our theme, Theologizing, are *theos* and *logos*. They are impregnated with mystery and the history of their interpretation runs from the twilight stories of gods and spirits in the mind of primitive peoples to the blazing light of revelation in the living and true God manifested in Jesus Christ.

Theology means the *science of God*, but not in the sense of modern rationalist investigation, though there have always been schoolmen theologians who have killed the reality and dynamism of living theology by their rationalist approach.

It rather means the *knowledge of God*, bearing in mind that in the Bible knowledge is a profoundly intimate and experienced reality. When Adam *knew* Eve it indicates a knowing of a sexual and spiritual order. The *conception* which resulted was a living being.

Theology is the knowledge of God which is deep, intimate and life-giving. It has its roots in the feeling dimension of the soul confronted with the mystery of the life which indwells all things and is transcendent above them. The word is one which has haunted me from the time I first recognized it, for its reality goes back much further than my recognition of the word, and its implications reach out to cosmic proportions that are beyond my furthest horizons.

There was first of all what I would call *intuitive theology*. This involves an exploration of the mind through the senses. As a young boy I wandered around the coastland of south-west Wales by day and by night and through the changing seasons. The heave and swell of the sea, the rise and fall of the wind, the morning and evening sun and the waxing and waning moon – all these gave me a *sense* of a pulsing, throbbing life within and between myself and the created order which constituted the mystery I later called God.

When I was twelve years of age I came to a moment of conversion in which I recognized and confessed Jesus Christ as my Saviour, Friend and Brother. This was the beginning of *living theology*. I interpreted the earlier sense of mystery and numinous, pervasive life in the context of the biblical revelation and the person of Jesus. I compared my natural, intuitive theology of childhood with my meeting with Jesus in experience and in the gospels and with the great conversion and confrontation stories of the patriarchs, prophets and apostles in Scripture. This led me to a serious application of mind and heart in *learning theology*.

Because my experience was so rich and my mind was so eager to learn more I began to read not only the basic theological texts of Scripture and liturgy but the writings of theologians, and began to develop a critical sense.

I felt a call to ministry within the Church of God and began formal theological education and soon discovered, especially in the Western Church, that theologians were not necessarily believers, and their influence sometimes had a deadening effect on the study of theology both in lecture room and pulpit.

Nevertheless I had some theological teachers who made the subject exciting and demanding. It was St Theresa of the Child Jesus who said: "If I had been a priest I should have made a thorough study of Hebrew and Greek so as to understand the thought of God as he has vouchsafed to express it in our human language."

The exciting and creative dimension of theological study was stimulated for me especially by the lecturers in Hebrew and New Testament Greek in Zürich and by the Professor of Dogmatic Theology in Edinburgh. I couldn't keep up with them in an academic sense but I can remember the exhilaration of anticipating them in an experiential sense. I was encouraged, corrected, chastised and confounded by the scale of disciplines that go to make up a basic theological education. When it came to selecting a topic of study for my post-graduate thesis I found in Thomas Merton a man who held together doctrine, experience and loving social concern in a contemplative theology that has undergirded me ever since.

With Merton my sense of *exploring theology* was confirmed and given clear direction. It was seeing and sharing the experience of God in the Church, in the contemplative dimension of world faiths and in the very stuff of ordinary human life that embraces every man, woman and child.

Theology is everywhere, and simple human experience and love is the end of a golden string which, when followed, leads to other and deeper aspects of the tender mercy of God.

Next I would mention *preaching theology*. When I went to the Episcopal Theological College in Edinburgh I led a series of lectures on homiletics and sermon construction. In a practical session one of the ordinands said that he had never heard a sermon that had held or even interested him. I questioned such a statement only to have every member of the class agree with him, maintaining stoutly that they had never heard an interesting sermon. In my previous Baptist background the sermon was the high point in the service, and though I have heard many boring, repetitive, badly-reasoned and ill-constructed sermons, I have also been enchanted by preachers who have held the congregation spellbound for an hour or more.

If a preacher is able to communicate theology by preaching then happy is that congregation. For me, there is little to compare with preaching theology, whether it be to a congregation of a thousand in an evangelistic rally or to a dozen faithful people at an early morning eucharist, though style and length may be very different. There is great joy (and danger) in being able to hold a congregation in the palm of your hand and a deep sense of responsibility must accompany such a ministry. The pattern for such a ministry is found in Christ in the midst of his amazed disciples as he unfolded the meaning of his risen life in the context of the prophetic word: "Then he opened their minds so they could understand the scriptures" (Luke 24:45).

When I come to *teaching theology* I recall Sunday afternoons in the Anglican chaplaincy in Glasgow when a group of students and others met with me around John Macquarrie's *Principles of Christian Theology*. We read and debated the doctrinal, experiential and moral implications of each chapter with great earnestness (not without humour), enjoying the cut and thrust of theological dialogue, followed by tea and cathedral evensong. I also think of the more recent one-to-one or group sharing of theology and New Testament Greek with novices within the Society of St Francis and the many opportunities of teaching theology within and extending from our Anglican Franciscan Order.

When in retrospect I feel again the excitement and dynamic of such creative theological sharing I wonder what I am doing living in a hermitage in the middle of fields with sheep and cattle! At such times I rather hope that my time in solitude, precious as it is, will be a three-year stint after the pattern of Elijah at the brook Cherith.

I say that tongue in cheek, for I do realize that I am *doing theology* here in living a life of prayer, study, work and writing for myself and for others. I take the material of everyday living in this place and relate it to the manifestation of God in the ordinary and extraordinary moments of my days and nights, sharing such theologizing with you in my prayer and writing.

My expectation of you as the reader is to take the seemingly disparate elements of *your* life and make theological sense of them, for there is nothing in human experience that is not grist to the theological mill. These may include the immense joy of spontaneous play with your own precious child, the exhilaration of intimate sexual relationship with your spouse, the satisfaction of a creative task in gardening, pottery or music-making or the wrestling with the confrontation of the love of God and the horrific Jewish holocaust.

As a result of such theological exploration you will sometimes be thrust into an experience of cosmic hope and charismatic joy and sometimes into an abyss of darkness and perplexity. But if you continue to explore, and relate the experiences of your life and relationships upon a wider theological canvas, then a picture will emerge encompassing the light and darkness and all the colour and texture of a life lived in the presence and mystery of God.

Response

* Have you recognized that the very ordinary happenings of daily life may be for you the very material of theology when considered prayerfully?

* Do you spend any time during the week specifically reading and learning theology alone or with a group?

* Take a particular day and record in your journal some of the incidents and meetings, exploring possible theological meaning relevant to such encounters.

The Arena of God's Creative Love

The world of theology is an exciting, mysterious, intelligible and yet also an incomprehensible world. *Credo ut intelligam* – I believe in order that I may understand. It is the science and knowledge of God which is so profound that its depths cannot be plumbed and so sublime that its heights cannot be attained. It is a world filled with ancient languages, creative wisdom, logical propositions and intuitive mysteries. Begin to believe and all the promises of faith are possible; begin to doubt, and amazingly, you are in debate with the wisdom of the ages. The world of theology is the arena of God's creative love, and once you have entered that arena there is no escape . . .

DAY THIRTY-EIGHT

Evangelizing

SCRIPTURE: Acts 2:37–47. The attraction of the gospel life

Prayer

We give you thanks, heavenly Father, for the mysterious life of your Holy Spirit in the works of creation, for the restless yearning you have planted within the human heart and for the love revealed to us in the gospel of the Lord Jesus. Give us grace to bear witness to all these blessings, that men and women may be drawn to the community of your Church by the evidence of vitality and joy among your people; Through Jesus Christ our Lord. Amen.

Reflection

When I was a teenage Christian with a real evangelical experience but often with more zeal than knowledge, I used to stand in a ring with other like-minded evangelists at hell-fire corner in Swansea opposite the old Rum and Punch pub and harangue the drunks on Saturday nights. We did some good, though the effect of throwing Bible-texts at tipsy characters was sometimes counter-productive. One chauvinist fellow looked at me over his pint one evening and assured me that there could be no women in heaven. When I queried this puzzling conclusion he quoted Revelation 8:1 which states that there will be silence in heaven for the space of half an hour!

251

Then sunny Saturday afternoons would find me with Rosie and her accordion leading a score or more children down to the beach. There we would hold an evangelistic service with choruses, stories and prayers followed by games and a dip in the sea. All this to the delight of many scores of children and parents. These were my attempts at evangelism.

Much more extreme was the behaviour of the twenty-year-old Antony of Egypt in the fourth century when he heard in church the words of Matthew 19:21: "If you would be perfect, go and sell all that you have and give to the poor; and come, follow me." He gave away his inheritance and went penniless into the desert in solitude for twenty years.

As a result of his life written by St Anthanasius "there arose monasteries even in the mountains, and the desert was made a city by monks coming out from their own and enrolling themselves in the heavenly city." Athanasius' story became an evangelistic tract setting crowds on fire for God and the life of prayer.

It seems at first sight that the apostle Peter, standing before the diverse peoples in Jerusalem on the day of Pentecost, preaching the gospel with boldness and fervour, was more akin to the kind of evangelistic endeavour first described above than that communicated by Antony following Jesus into the desert to a life of prayer. But if you will examine the whole of our reading you will see that there is a quality of mystery and life among the believers that itself drew the crowds, which was prior to and underlying the proclamation.

First of all there was a tarrying period in Jerusalem waiting for the coming of the Holy Spirit, for proclamation without such an anointing would have fallen to the ground or caused an unholy riot. Then there was the baptism in the Holy Spirit which imparted not only holiness but power to proclaim the crucified and risen Christ.

As a result of such proclamation the people were cut to the heart and cried out under the convicting power of the Spirit in repentance and faith. They were baptized into Christ among the company of believers and we are given a beautiful description of the manner of life of the early believers which became an incandescent beacon to the world around:

> They devoted themselves to the apostles' teaching and to the fellowship, to the breaking of bread and to prayer. Everyone was filled with awe, and many wonders and miraculous signs were done by the apostles. All the believers were together and had everything in common. Selling their possessions and goods, they gave to anyone as he had need. Every day they continued to meet together in the temple courts. They broke bread in their homes and ate together with glad and sincere hearts, praising God and enjoying the favour of all the people. And the Lord added to their number daily those who were being saved. (Acts 2:42–47)

The *teaching* concerned the love that became incarnate at Bethlehem and Calvary; the *fellowship* was the experience of indwelling and overflow of the joy of the Holy Spirit; the *breaking of bread* consisted not only of the sharing of Christ's body and blood in communion but the common joy of ordinary meals in the generosity of love, and the *prayers* constituted the network of adoration and intercession that fired the early Church in its pentecostal life.

The effect of such a radiant and vibrant witness was not unlike the effect brought about by St Athanasius' description of the flaming love and zeal for God portrayed in the life of Antony surrendering himself to God in the desert. Peoples' hearts were stirred and thousands were drawn towards such a manifestation of the Holy Spirit.

I carry the tensions of these two poles of evangelism within my own heart – the evangelism of proclamation and the evangelism of a life poured out for God in the desert. It would be foolish for me to deny that I miss the excitement and dynamism of proclamation-evangelism, the cut and thrust of friendly dialogue and persuasion with its attendant learning from those with whom Christ is shared.

But I am also aware of the evangelism of the hidden and interior life. I have found that people in our frenetic and workaholic society have parched and dried-out souls so that when they sense the moisture, and then the living waters that are abundant in the hidden springs of the desert, they long to know more of such places of refreshment.

I have been joyfully surprised, in seeking to share Christ with those of other traditions, to find him already there, reverenced with a depth and breadth not often found among Christians. Take these words from Martin Buber, the Hasidic Jewish philosopher:

> From my youth onwards I have found in Jesus my great brother. That Christianity has regarded and does regard him as God and Saviour has always appeared to me as a fact of the highest importance which for his sake and my own I must endeavour to understand . . . My own fraternally open relationship to him has grown even stronger and dearer, and today I see him more strongly and clearly than ever before. I am more than ever certain that a great place belongs to him in Israel's history of faith and that this place cannot be described by any of the usual categories.

It is not our task to wage an evangelistic war on those who do not say the same words as we do. Rather, aware of the treasure we have found in the gospel and of the living Christ who has called and saved us, we must be gentle in our sharing, expecting to find in those hidden and unusually new situations in which we find ourselves, the cosmic and universal Christ.

If our evangelism is based on duty, fear or fanaticism it will not only be counter-productive but in the end will lead us through exclusivism to religious intolerance and hardness of heart in which we lose the very Christ we set out to proclaim.

Love is the only motive for evangelism, and love is the only content of our message. The wonderful thing is that if evangelism is seen in the context of sharing, then true dialogue takes place. You listen to the truth spoken from the heart of the other, and share your understanding of God's love in Christ. And suddenly, Christ appears, first in the love which overflows the other's heart and then between you both as the One who promised: "Where two or three are gathered in my name, there am I in the midst of them."

So wherever we are – in the busy activity of marketplace, hospital, school, home, job centre or in a hermitage in a plum orchard surrounded by fields and solitude, evangelism is an overflowing of the heart of love in prayer and in words, in speech and in silence. To such an overflow of love people are drawn, and transformed. And, in turn, they will radiate that same love.

Response

* Write into your journal three definitions of evangelism that you find current in the contemporary religious climate.

* Write your own definition. Reflect upon its motivation and ask yourself what feelings it evokes in your heart towards those who do not share your faith.

* Select a particular day this week, setting aside fifteen minutes of silence before God in the morning. Then allow God's love to flow through you in whatever ways open up.

At the end of the day record incidents, meetings and conversations.

Gandhi on Christ

I believe that he belongs not only to Christianity but to the entire world, to all races and people; it matters little under what flag, name or doctrine they may work, profess a faith, or worship a God inherited from their ancestors.

MAHATMA GANDHI

DAY THIRTY-NINE

Belonging

SCRIPTURE: 1 Corinthians 12:12–26. Belonging together

Prayer

You have made us for yourself, O Lord, and implanted within our hearts a yearning for your love; Confirm in us that sense of belonging to you so that in tribulation and distress as well as in joy and blessedness we may always trust in your mercy and find in you our peace;
Through Jesus Christ our Lord. Amen.

Reflection

Some years ago a girls' school near Poole in Dorset wanted a friar to spend a week circulating the classes and sharing in assembly, teaching and informal dialogue. I accepted the invitation, staying with one of the staff and enjoying a week of warm-hearted and good-humoured sharing with quite moving moments of friendship and openness.

One morning the senior teacher left me with about twenty sixth-form girls for an hour of mutual talk on "personal relationships". The idea was that I would give about twenty minutes of input and then open it up for discussion. Before I did any talking we listened to one of my favourite tracks from Carole King's LP *Tapestry*. It was the song "You've Got a Friend", written for her by James Taylor, and all the girls knew it:

When you're down and troubled
And you need some loving care,
And nothing, nothing is going right,
Close your eyes and think of me
And soon I will be there
To brighten up even your darkest night.

You just call out my name
And you know wherever I am
I'll come running to see you again;
Winter, Spring, Summer or Fall,
All you have to do is call
And I'll be there –
    You've got a Friend.

We listened quietly, with some of the girls gently singing along. Then I talked about the way in which the lover was saying to the loved one: "Whatever happens, in joy or sorrow, when things are good or bad, if everyone turns against you and there's nowhere for you to go – just call me and I'll always come – for I love you."

I'd got to know some of the girls by this time, and I looked around the circle. "Have any of you known a relationship of complete trust like that?" I asked.

One of the humorous, extrovert girls grinned and said: "Well, I certainly can't say that about my boy-friend – *he's* not to be trusted!" We all laughed, and then suddenly one of the girls said: "Yes, I can say that. My boy-friend is just like the song, and we completely trust one another." The response was immediate and the whole discussion became animated with nearly everyone chipping in. Then something extremely funny happened.

I was broadening the discussion into wider relationships and said: "In just under a week we've developed a particularly warm relationship between ourselves, haven't we? That's happened because of your willingness to accept me and my wanting to reach you. But supposing I had come into the group this morning snooty and sitting on my high horse, and one of you had made one of your funny remarks which I thought offended my dignity, and I turned to you and said severely: 'Don't you *dare* to speak to me like that . . .' "

As I was saying this the school cook passed the long window, looking in as she did so. She saw me point at the girl as I said these words, and immediately looked away, quickened her step and got out of sight as fast as she could.

The whole class looked aghast, and some girls put their hands to their mouths in consternation. "Oh," said one of them, "she thought it was for real." "Yes," I grinned, "she did!"

It was a gift of illustration and the rest of the period flew by – they said it was the best lesson they'd had for a long time. I was very amused but also moved to see the way in which a deputation went up to the cook at lunch time and explained that what she had seen was not what had actually happened, so concerned that she did not get it wrong.

It was an exercise in human relationships, a sense of belonging, and it was clear that "belonging together" affected us all, personally and corporately, in our loving relationships at all levels.

Belonging assured us of a "place" in the scheme of things and we felt that it delivered us from fear of isolation and loneliness from infancy to old age – "Nice thing if you can get it," we said, realizing that many people live and die without it.

That was almost ten years ago and I've prayed this morning for that whole group, for most of them must be married with families of their own now – and I'm sure that whenever they've heard Carole King again they've remembered that lesson.

This sense of belonging and of having a place and a

meaning is implanted deep within us all. It is not simply a matter of coming in from the cold of fear or isolation. It is a positive feeling of loving and being loved. I've put that the wrong way round, for we cannot love unless we are loved ourselves.

One of the other songs I had on cassette with "You've got a Friend", was the Beatles' "Eleanor Rigby". It tells of the loneliness of a girl who lived and died in one room and of the parallel isolation of a priest who darned his socks and wrote his sermons alone. Father Mackenzie conducted Eleanor's funeral, wiping the earth from his hands as he left her grave, while the sad refrain continues: "All the lonely people, where do they all come from? All the lonely people, where do they all belong?"

One of the sad marks of our present market economy society is the idea that everything/everyone has a price, as if we could all wear economic price-tags. Almost the worst thing to say about anything or anyone is that they are uneconomic. That is why unemployed people often feel themselves to be of little value – not needed, not belonging – and it makes them eventually feel unloved.

The value of a person does not lie in his salary or her professional role or expertise. Love is not economic but arises spontaneously out of the depths of our humanity (and our animality), as a free gift of grace. It is only as people feel themselves loved that they can respond to relationships at all, let alone feel their inherent worth as human beings and potential children of God.

If this is true on a human level it is certainly true in the life of the spirit. "We love him because he first loved us," says the apostle John, for the only real spiritual life is the one which arises from a stirring of love within the human heart by the Spirit of God. Religion which is composed of rules and regulations, of moral codes, external rites and religious duties, is as chilling as the bureaucracy that surrounds it.

But a faith which is interior and grounded in the love of God in Christ is like an inward spring which floods all the crevices of the soul and overflows in an attitude of compassion in the world and continual acts of practical concern in society. There are only two commandments – love for God and neighbour – and they are both one.

Belonging means primarily belonging to God because you are loved by him, belonging to our common humanity because he has placed you there and belonging to the created order because of the interrelated web and pattern within the cosmos. Because we belong we have a place and we have responsibilities. We accept our place and give place to others. We are loved and we love, therefore the love returns to us again.

There are people in our society who have never felt welcomed or loved as children, have never made any mark at school, have not been fulfilled in their job, have drifted from job to job or never been employed at all. With such a background they have not been creative in marriage, and home has not therefore been conducive to starting their children off on the right foot.

Yet at each of those milestones there has been the possibility of meeting others who have belonged, who have felt affirmed and loved and who can stimulate warmth and joy to their fellows as channels of peace in the Franciscan sense.

We may have lost the tribal sense of corporate identity found among primitive peoples as well as the community sense and wider family groupings which were a part of our own society until recently, but if we can affirm the love that dwells in the human heart as a reflection of the love of God, then we can find the sense of belonging at its source.

The solidarity of the human race is in the love of God, and no one is an island because we are all connected in the deepest places of our psyche. To love is to belong and to belong promotes neighbourliness, friendship, sharing and hospitality.

Our reading today depicts the Church as the Body of Christ and each of us as members of that body – rejoicing together and suffering together, bearing and sharing one another's joys and sorrows. If this pattern were truly lived out in the Church, then our denominational barriers would crumble and profound questions would be asked at a deeper level and in a different climate. I have Christian friends to whom I belong and who belong to me who are Pentecostal, Catholic, Baptist, Methodist, Orthodox, Presbyterian, Brethren and even Anglican! If belonging to God and to one another was more often and more clearly lived out, then the pattern of the Body of Christ would be a pattern for the whole world.

When our Lord returns in glory then the unity of his love will be manifested in the reconciliation of all things in heaven and on earth (Ephesians 1:19–23), and we shall truly belong in the communion of saints and God will be all in all (1 Corinthians 15:28).

But why not begin to live out this belonging today, not only on the basis of fellowship in Christ with those you recognize as belonging to his Body, but with all those you meet on the basis of our common humanity. For we all need each other in the fellowship of love.

Response

* Record a particular experience in which you have felt a positive sense of belonging and sharing within a relationship or group.

* Record a particular experience in which you have felt excluded or lacking a sense of belonging and sharing within a relationship or group.

Belonging

* If your sense of belonging is secure, extend hospitality
to others in terms of friendship, home and church and
make the first move today.

Belonging

As the bridegroom to his chosen,
    as the king unto his realm,
As the keep unto the castle,
    as the pilot to the helm,
So, Lord, are you to me.

As the fountain in the garden,
    as the candle in the dark,
As the treasure in the coffer,
    as the manna in the ark,
So, Lord, are you to me.

As the music at the banquet,
    as the stamp unto the seal,
As the medicine to the fainting,
    as the wine-cup at the meal,
So, Lord, are you to me.

As the ruby in the setting,
    as the honey in the comb,
As the light within the lantern,
    as the parent in the home,
So, Lord, are you to me.

As the sunshine in the heavens,
    as the image in the glass,
As the fruit unto the fig-tree,
    as the dew unto the grass,
So, Lord, are you to me.

Paraphrase from JOHN TAULER

265

DAY FORTY

Epilogue – Returning

SCRIPTURE: Mark 9:14–29. Down in the valley

Prayer

Upon the mountain you were transfigured in light, Lord Jesus, and drew your disciples into your heavenly glory; down in the valley you led them to humble service and compassionate healing.
Grant us periods of communion in prayer and adoration, and then lead us into the dark places of our world to shed light and hope among those who need your love;
To the glory and praise of your saving name. Amen.

Reflection

I have not been writing for hermits! Your reading of this book has probably been part of the prayer and study aspect of your life, and I am aware that most of my readers are actively involved in the Church and the world, leading busy lives and wishing they had more time for prayer and quiet.

Today's theme of Returning presumes that there is some mountain-top experience to return from, and that the contemplative dimension, though less than you would wish it to be, is part of your commitment to God. Our spheres of ministry may be quite different and both of us need continual discernment and openness of attitude towards the will of God to know where the future direction lies.

When I came to this place of solitude and prayer with the encouragement of The Society of St Francis I came open-endedly. By the time this book is published I shall be into my third year and my caravan may have given way to a stone cell or wooden hut. It may be that I shall continue this kind of life of prayer, solitude and writing described in this book for some years to come. But I need constant discernment and awareness of what God is saying to me, and I shall need guidance from my spiritual director and from my community as I seek to live in simplicity and obedience.

As I look towards the great tradition of prayer I find that though some of the desert fathers and mothers remained in the wilderness, others had fellowship with other monks, nuns and monasteries. In the Celtic tradition there was a kind of alternating life of contemplation and preaching – a ministry of peregrination and pilgrimage in which St Columba, St David, St Patrick prayed, founded churches, preached, worked with their hands, went off to a solitary island and returned again.

Though Antony of Egypt went into the desert for twenty years he then organized a community of hermits and actively supported the Nicene party in the Arian controversy, returning at last to his hermitage. St Seraphim, after thirty years as a forest hermit, returned to a monastery cell and for the last eight years of his life devoted his energies to giving spiritual counsel, with a constant stream of penitents coming to him from all parts of Russia.

Although there are hermits in the Franciscan tradition together with the contemplative life of the Poor Clares, St Francis himself lived a combination of a deep life of prayer and of active preaching and witness. Franciscan spirituality embraces profound commitment to both prayer and service. So I need discernment for my future pattern, as you do for yours.

Our reading today occurs immediately after the Transfiguration of Christ upon the mountain and is the story of the exorcism and healing of the epileptic boy, followed by Jesus' prediction of his own death. The same pattern is found in the three synoptic gospels spelling out an incarnation theology. The Transfiguration depicts Christ's pre-natal glory with the Father; the valley of service depicts the life and ministry of Jesus on earth and the prediction of his passion points in the direction of Calvary.

In our own experience this may serve as a model of life in Christ. The Transfiguration symbolizes the mountain of contemplative prayer; the valley opens out into a ministry of teaching and healing; the prediction includes the constant dying of the old ego to sin and self and the acknowledgement of our mortality which leads to eternal life.

I have stressed in all my writings the need of every Christian, indeed of every human being, to develop a dimension of contemplation, for without it we do not attain to a real humanity. Nevertheless we cannot stay upon the mountain for there is a valley of need which calls for positive and practical service to the needy. This valley of service lies between the deepening life of prayer and the valley of the shadow of death which is before us all. Beyond that is eternal glory, but our present concern must be with our world and its need.

Things may have been different in earlier times, but with our contemporary vivid and immediate consciousness of universal human need it is clear that no Christian can remain unaware or unmoved by the immense problems of our day. Famine, nuclear war, the arms trade, terrorism, political oppression and disintegration, torture and ecological pollution – these are all on the social agenda for the Christian. Any teaching which propagates a flight into a world of meditation ignoring these problems and treating contemplation as a "flight of the alone to the Alone" is neither Christian nor human. A world-denying religion

268

which ignores basic human values and problems lies at one extreme and a social gospel which has no contemplative base at the other. Neither is acceptable.

The danger of an other-worldly spirituality is that it does not take *this* world seriously enough. It can appear in many forms, sometimes as a "pie in the sky when you die" attitude, or in an eastern interpretation of this world as merely *maya* and therefore unreal so that no ethical or moral demands are made. But I would hasten to add that it is encouraging to witness the social awareness in Hinduism of the continued traditions of Mahatma Gandhi and the Ramakrishna Society with its medical and care concerns, and of the contemporary Buddhist witness to peace and justice.

The danger of the hyper-active social gospellers is that the lack of a contemplative base can lead to what I would call caring depression or compassion fatigue. This is a form of impotence brought about by the immensity of the problems in the face of inadequate resources or bureaucratic red tape. This, in turn, can lead to reactive anger erupting in violence and destruction.

I don't have any easy remedy to the problems I've just listed, which are compounded by the attendant greed and energy consumption of the "developed" world, but we can all test our lives by a basic gospel pattern which would ensure that we are contributing our part in the best way we can, leaving the ultimate result to God and not thinking that we have to shoulder all the problems of the world. I am presupposing that we are baptized Christians in fellowship with the Church and participating in word and sacrament. The pattern would then run something like this:

1 We should develop a personal and corporate life of contemplative prayer.
2 We should give attention to manual and mental work balanced in a healthy equilibrium.

3 We should reach out in friendship to people of other faiths and none – not to proselytize, but simply for friendship's sake and the widening of our human horizons.

4 We should commit ourselves according to our abilities by finance, time and energy to a peace and justice group such as Amnesty International, Campaign for the Abolition of Torture, Campaign Against the Arms Trade and relief agencies, etc. There are also peace movements in most of the major denominations, and they are linked to each other.

5 All these things come together in the exercise of personal *discernment*, for if you can find *your* place then you will remain positive and effective and be saved from depression or unproductive anger.

The result of embracing a disciplined pattern also releases an element of spontaneity and freshness in your life with an availability to God that may cause a personal spiritual revolution. Perhaps in a year or two you will find yourself considering things beyond your present imagining.

As a family you may find yourselves opening your home to one or two foster children or giving hospitality on a regular basis to handicapped or lonely people; as a young couple you may feel you could offer a few years to a missionary society or an overseas aid programme; as an individual you may feel a vocation to join the helpers of Mother Teresa of Calcutta or the Little Brothers and Sisters of Jesus. It may be on a school governing body or in direct political and social action that you can make your contribution, or perhaps you will be drawn to offer yourself for ordination or as a reader or local preacher in your church, parish or circuit. All these are possible ways to return to the marketplace of witness which may be an overspill of your basic Christian discipleship and prayer.

How can you know God's leading in any of these things? Well, if you belong to a sensitive church or group, part of its charism should be discernment and prophecy according to the New Testament pattern:

> While they were worshipping the Lord and fasting, the Holy Spirit said, "Set apart for me Barnabas and Saul for the work to which I have called them." So after they had fasted and prayed, they placed their hands on them and sent them off. (Acts 13:2f.)

It is the Spirit who guides, speaks and empowers, and it is the Spirit who grants discernment to a person and a community. But if you face the problems, fill the gaps, rush into service, expend your energies – all without first ascending the mountain of prayer and transfiguration – you will find yourself impotent and frustrated as were the disciples in the valley who were vainly trying their own methods until Jesus descended with the chosen three disciples.

You can only return to the valley if you have first ascended the mountain.

Response

* Reflect upon the fivefold pattern of discipleship listed in this chapter. Write down your response under each heading.

* From such a response, can you trace a balance of prayer and action in your life?

* If you are part of a functioning family, does the pattern of your life involve or exclude the other members? If single, is your life balanced between necessary solitude and shared fellowship?

Love the Whole World

Let not men's sin dishearten you; love a man even in his sin, for that love is a likeness of the divine love, and is the summit of love on earth. Love all God's creation, both the whole and every grain of sand. Love every leaf, every ray of light. Love the animals, love the plants, love each separate thing. If you love each thing you will perceive the mystery of God in all; and when once you perceive this, you will thenceforward grow every day to a fuller understanding of it: until you come at last to love the whole world with a love that will be all-embracing and universal.

DOSTOEVSKY

ACKNOWLEDGEMENTS

The author is grateful for permission to use the following material:

Poem *The Penalty of Love* by S. R. Lysaght. London:
Macmillan & Co Ltd.

St Francis' story from *The Fioretti* from *Omnibus of the Sources
for the Life of St Francis*, edited by Marion A. Habig.
London: SPCK.

Trigger in Europe by William Holt. London: Michael Joseph.

Prayer by Etta Gullick from *It's Me O Lord* by Michael Hollings
and Etta Gullick. Southend: Mayhew McCrimmon.

Story from *The Wisdom of the Desert* by Thomas Merton. New
York: New Directions.

Quotation from *The Way of Holiness* by Robert Van de Weyer.
London: Fount Paperbacks.

Poem *To Keep a True Lent* by Robert Herrick (died 1674).

Quotation from *Blues in the Night* by Lionel Blue. London: BBC
Publications.

'Body Sensations' from *Sadhana* by Anthony de Mello. New
York: Image Books (Doubleday).

Quotation from *Brother Edward: Priest and Evangelist*. London:
Hodder & Stoughton.

Song *People Who Need People*.

Quotation from *The Four Loves* by C. S. Lewis. London: Fount
Paperbacks.

Quotations from *The Duncton Chronicles* by William Horwood.
London: Hamlyn Books (Hutchinson Publishing Group).

Poem 'The Gambler' by G. A. Studdert Kennedy from *The
Unutterable Beauty*. London: Hodder & Stoughton.

Quotation from *Contemplative Prayer* by Thomas Merton.
London: Darton, Longman and Todd.

Quotations from *Jung and the Story of Our Time* by Laurens
van der Post. London: The Hogarth Press.

Quotation from Carl G. Jung, *Collected Works*. London:
Routledge & Kegan Paul Ltd.

St Francis' quotation from *Saint Francis of Assisi* by Omer Englebert. London: Burns & Oates.

Lines from Gilbert and Sullivan's *Patience*.

Prayer from *Prayers of Life* by Michel Quoist. Dublin: Gill & Macmillan.

Prayer of Ramon Lull quoted in *Fool of Love* by E. Allison Peers. London: SCM Press.

Words from *From This Day Forward* by Madeleine L'Engle. New York: Dell Publishing; Oxford: Lion Publishing.

The Gift of Tears by Isaac the Syrian (died 700).

'Jubilus' by Jacopone da Todi in *Jacopone da Todi* by Evelyn Underhill. London: Dent.

Words of St Romauld quoted in *Perfect Fools* by John Saward. Oxford: Oxford University Press.

Words of Albert Einstein in an article in *The New York Post* in 1972.

Quotation from *A Question of Conscience* by Charles Davies. London: Hodder & Stoughton.

Quotations from *Good Daughters* by Mary Hocking. London: Chatto and Windus.

Quotations from 'The Golden Globe Contest', in *Quest for Adventure* by Chris Bonington. London: Hodder & Stoughton.

Words of Thomas Merton from *The School of Charity: The Letters of Thomas Merton*, edited by Patrick Hart. New York: Farrar, Straus & Giroux.

Words from lyrics of *Sonny Boy*.

Poem *I Remember* by Thomas Hood, found in *Palgrave's Golden Treasury*.

Words from *Walking to Jerusalem* by Gerard Hughes. London: Darton, Longman & Todd.

Words of Mahatma Gandhi, source unknown.

Words from lyrics of 'You've Got a Friend' written by James Taylor for Carole King's LP *Tapestry*.

Paraphrase from John Tauler (died 1361), hymn in *Hymns for Today* No. 7.

Quotation from Dostoevsky, *The Brothers Karamazov*. Harmondsworth: Penguin Books.